The Psychology
of
Vocational Choice

A BLAISDELL BOOK IN PSYCHOLOGY

Raymond G. Kuhlen, *Syracuse University*

CONSULTING EDITOR

JOHN L. HOLLAND

The
Psychology
of
Vocational Choice

A THEORY OF PERSONALITY TYPES
AND MODEL ENVIRONMENTS

BLAISDELL PUBLISHING COMPANY
A DIVISION OF GINN AND COMPANY
Waltham, Massachusetts · Toronto · London

DESIGNED BY
Larry Kamp *and* Barbara Liman

Foreword

A SUCCESSFUL EDUCATIONAL PROGRAM must necessarily be based solidly on an understanding of the psychology of the learner and the learning process. And the application of psychological principles and theory to the educative process may well represent the major point of impact of psychological science upon society. But psychology is a complex discipline, made up of a variety of subdisciplines and characterized by a diversity of viewpoints. Many of the subdisciplines—the psychology of learning, developmental psychology, social psychology, clinical psychology—have much to offer the educator, but the avenues through which their contributions may be brought to a focus on education are often obscure. Oftentimes it is difficult for an instructor to find a standard text that is suitable for the course *he* wishes to teach. Although he may well be aware of the diversity of material available, he often lacks a ready means of giving students access to authoritative specialized summaries interpreted for educational practice. Paperback volumes, each dealing with a limited topic and available at low per unit cost, permit the instructor to supplement his "standard" text at points where he wishes greater emphasis or strength, or to select coordinated paperback volumes to constitute the "text" with the particular emphasis he desires.

The books to be published in this series will, of course, deal mainly with the standard areas of educational psychology— human development, learning, adjustment, and statistics and measurement. Where special and different viewpoints exist in particular areas, different types of books will be made available. However, the series is planned as an open-ended publishing venture. As occasion arises, books will be presented dealing with special problems (for example, school integration, vocational choice) with which educators must be concerned and to the solution of which psychologists can contribute. The series is also viewed as an appropriate vehicle by means of which a psychologist in any area of specialization may address himself to educators, and as a means by which directors of major research programs may summarize and interpret their findings for educational applications. When utilized for this purpose, a series of this kind may hopefully reduce "cultural lag," making results of research programs or theoretical developments more readily and quickly a part of the instructional material in educational psychology. In such instances the significance of the material and the relevance of the topic to education will be the main consideration in the decision to publish rather than possible use as text material.

In total, a paperback series represents an extremely flexible means of meeting varied instructional purposes. The books in this series are written to serve the needs of both preservice teachers and in-service teachers, but in a broad sense are addressed to the professional education community. The range of titles now in preparation are listed elsewhere in this volume.

RAYMOND G. KUHLEN

Preface

I HAVE WRITTEN this short book to present a theory of vocational behavior, a theory I have found useful. I hope practitioners, researchers, and students will also find it useful. And although I have written primarily for a student and professional audience, I have tried to write so that an intelligent person can, without much difficulty, find the principal ideas clear and helpful.

The theory was developed to integrate the burgeoning literature of vocational choice, vocational stability, and vocational achievement; to suggest new research; and to outline some of the practical applications of our current knowledge. Most of the evidence that supports the theory has been reported earlier in journals and monographs. The major findings in these studies have been summarized here, along with some new research and relevant vocational literature. However, because I am primarily interested in presenting a theory, not in citing the supporting evidence, the reader should consult textbooks and other reviews of the literature for more complete accounts.

The impetus for my work came partly from my dissatisfaction with current thinking about vocational behavior. To put it bluntly, theoretical formulations about vocational behavior have usually been truisms concerning personal development and vocations. These clichés can be applied to all behavior; they lack *content* and so cannot be subjected to scientific examination: for example, "Vocational choice is developmental." So, one might add, is the choice of a wife or a dog. Again: "Vocational choice is the implementation of a self-concept." But which self-concepts lead to which choices? In short, typical theoretical statements about vocational choice have been unspecific and devoid of definitions and psychological content.

I also saw that the need for a way to synthesize our vocational knowledge is acute and growing. Although the empirical research of the past has provided useful knowledge, that knowledge consists largely of endless specific pieces of information obtained from the use of aptitude tests and interest inventories that usually lack an explicit rationale. Satisfactory integrative theories are not available. These formless data must be interpreted and reinterpreted—a formidable task—by every investigator, teacher, and student. The advent of the computer has merely increased our need for theory, because empiricism is now galloping rather than plodding.

My biases about the role that theory plays in research are several. First, I feel that we must make an effort to construct theories of vocational behavior; otherwise, we will continue to wander aimlessly through our data and the correlates of our favorite tests. Because most workers have been intimidated by the philosophers of science, we have made only limited attempts at theorizing. And because in our attempts at constructing theories we have felt it necessary to satisfy criteria so strict that they are more appropriate to the next generation than to our own, we have often failed to come up with any theory at all. Second, I think our emphasis upon the trappings of science—mathematics and methods—has fostered the misconception that theories should be proposed only after careful, extensive planning.

In reality, constructing a theory is an exciting, creative task; it may or may not emerge from the application of a set of formal rules or procedures. Unfortunately, many researchers are still committed to the building-block tradition of science; they believe that carefulness, gradualness, and sincerity make up for insightful speculation.

I admit that I have frequently gone well beyond the data; however, I feel that there is as much risk in creeping empiricism as in idle speculation. Unfortunately, theories in social science are often viewed as targets for criticism and researchmanship rather than as intellectual tools that should be tried out for their usefulness in empirical work. We need, I think, to make greater use of theory as a tool in our problem solving and to give theory building a status equal to that of method and empiricism. In this matter, Darwin's words seem especially appropriate: "Without speculation, there is no good and original observation."

The present theory is only one attempt to organize and interpret our knowledge of vocational behavior. I hope it will lead to the creation of more useful theories. We need many more.

I am indebted to many friends and colleagues who have provided me with valuable counsel, criticism, and support. They include Alexander W. Astin, John O. Crites, Leonard D. Goodstein, Sandra W. Lutz, Willis D. Poland, John M. Stalnaker, and Richard R. Stephenson. I am also grateful to the series editor, Raymond Kuhlen, for his encouragement and skillful shaping of my work. Finally, I am especially indebted to Laura Kent for her ability to recast my writing into plain English. Although I can no longer accurately discriminate their ideas from my own or always remember their special contributions, I am in their debt for much of what is useful in the book. On the other hand, they are not responsible for my errors or my inability to use their insights.

JOHN L. HOLLAND

Iowa City, Iowa

Contents

Contents

CHAPTER ONE

Introduction to the Theory

ALL OF US are confronted with vocational decisions throughout our lives. We can escape such problems for brief periods, but they are rarely resolved once and for all. At each stage of life, we must cope with vocational questions: What do I want to be when I grow up? Should I become an engineer or an artist? Should I become an airline hostess or a secretary? I'm a good research engineer, but should I accept a supervisory job? I'm a good teacher, but would I be a good superintendent? Would I like it? Should I get out of teaching and sell textbooks? I have never been a good salesman; have I missed the boat somewhere? Can I adjust to being retired?

These and similar questions are what this book is about. It summarizes what we know about the choice of a vocation, and it presents a special way of organizing this knowledge for easier comprehension and use--in short, a theory.

The theory is primarily concerned with explaining how people make vocational choices, what leads them to change jobs or vocation, and what personal and environmental factors are conducive to vocational achievement. To a lesser degree, the theory is also concerned with personal development and personality.

Because the theory grows mainly out of the problems and concepts suggested by our current knowledge of vocational and nonvocational life, a discussion of certain background concepts will help the reader to understand the theory. This section de-

1

scribes our current knowledge, outlines some problems arising from the lack of organization of this knowledge, and explains the ideas and concepts that form the intellectual foundation of the theory. This section is followed by a summary of the theory itself.

BACKGROUND CONCEPTS

Our knowledge of the personal characteristics and situational forces related to the choice of a vocation has increased enormously in recent years. We have learned much about people by the use of vocational interest inventories and of inventories and devices for describing personality. At present, we know that a person's vocational interests and preferences are associated with a great range of personal and background information. This knowledge has led to several concepts and assumptions that underlie the theory.

The choice of a vocation is an expression of personality. For many years, it was popular to interpret a person's scores on vocational interest inventories and his choice of vocation as a function of his "vocational interests," as if these interests were different from or independent of personality. A long history of adherence to this concept produced an independent literature known as "interest measurement." The work of Berdie [13], Strong [121], Darley and Hagenah [27], and Super and Crites [124] epitomizes the view that interest inventories measure interests, vocational choices, and vocational preferences.

Growing knowledge about the personal and environmental factors associated with a person's vocational choice made explicit the need for a broader conception. This need became clearer when we learned that vocational preferences are sometimes moderately correlated with personality and originality scales [68], self-ratings on various personality traits, daydreams about future accomplishment, responses to certain projective devices, values and goals, attitudes of parents, and many other personal and situational forces. Various writers suggested the need for a more comprehensive view of vocational preferences and interests, although their statements were often tentative and limited: "interest inventory scores are measures of self-concept" [16], "vocational interest measurement is a special case in personality theory" [27], "vocational choice is the implementation of a self-concept" [125], and "vocational choice is developmental" [125]. Such statements imply that a person's vocational choice is the outcome of his life history and not a decision independent of his past life [106, 17].

If vocational preference is construed as an expression of personality, then "vocational interests" represent the expression of personality in work, hobbies, recreational activities, and preferences. In short, what we have called "vocational interests" are simply another aspect of personality. Just as we have developed theories of personality from our knowledge of sex, parental relationships, and behavior, so we can construct theories of personality from our knowledge of vocational life and reinterpret as an expression of personality what we have called "vocational interests."

Perhaps some examples will serve to make clear the meaning of this reinterpretation. If we think of vocational interests and personality as independent domains, we will regard "I like to use tools to build things" as an expression of interest but "I like to hit people with tools" as an expression of personality. Yet both statements tell us how the subject uses tools—constructively or destructively. To ignore the constructive use of tools and similar activities as an index of personality is to ignore about half of man's conscious life. To take another example, a "Yes" response to the item "I would like to be a women's clothing designer" is regarded as an interest item, but even a naïve person would regard "I like to wear women's clothes" (if answered "Yes" by a man) as an important sign of personal aberration, although the content of both items is similar.

Interest inventories are personality inventories. If vocational interests are an expression of personality, then it follows that interest inventories are personality inventories. Forer [40] was probably the first to develop an inventory to assess personality from interests and activities and to illustrate how a subject's responses to apparently neutral content (vocational interests and activities) could be interpreted as expressions of various dimensions of personality. Unfortunately, Forer did not put his ideas to a direct scientific test. He did, however, show that we can distinguish a great variety of psychiatric and medical groups by their scores on various scales of an interest inventory, the Kuder Preference Record [41].

Forer's theorizing led in part to the construction of Holland's *Vocational Preference Inventory* [63], a personality inventory composed entirely of occupational titles. Generally, scales were developed by hypothesizing that preferences for occupations are expressions of personality. The rationale for the development of the inventory contains a more complete statement of this hypothesis:

> The choice of an occupation is an expressive act which reflects the person's motivation, knowledge, personality, and ability. Occupations represent a way of life, an environment rather than a set of isolated work functions or skills. To work as a carpenter means not only to use tools but also to have a certain status, community role, and a special pattern of living. In this sense, the choice of an occupational title represents several kinds of information: the S's motivation, his knowledge of the occupation in question, his insight and understanding of himself, and his abilities. In short, item responses may be thought of as limited but useful expressive or projective protocols.

The individual scales for the fifth revision of the VPI have useful reliability and validity. And more important, the development and validation of the VPI make it clear that vocational preferences are indeed signs of various personality traits. Similar support for the concept has been provided by Garman [47], who used responses to the Strong Vocational Interest Blank to develop and validate a scale measuring anxiety.

To summarize, we have clear evidence that it is useful to interpret or construe what have been called vocational interest inventories as personality inventories. Moreover, the content of vocational interest inventories provides scales whose reliabilities and validities approximate those obtained for other methods.

Vocational stereotypes have reliable and important psychological and sociological meanings. In the same way that we judge people by their friends, dress, and actions, so we judge them by their vocations. Our everyday experience has generated a sometimes inaccurate but apparently useful knowledge of what people in various occupations are like. Thus we believe that plumbers are handy, lawyers aggressive, actors self-centered, salesmen persuasive, accountants precise, scientists unsociable, and the like. In earlier years, social scientists were skeptical of the accuracy of this amorphous folklore of vocational stereotypes (many still are!), but recent work makes it clear that many vocational stereotypes have some validity. Not only do people agree upon the stereotypes for a given vocation, but also scientific evidence gives support to some aspects of the stereotypes: lawyers *are* aggressive and scientists *are* unsociable [11, 56, 69, 105, 123].

The assumption that vocational stereotypes have reliable psychological and sociological meanings is important, because most interest inventories rest heavily on its validity. If vocational stereotypes were unreliable and inaccurate, the validity of interest inventories would be seriously reduced. In the case of the present theory, the validity of this assumption lends credence to the first assumption—vocational choice is an expression of personality—and to several subsequent assumptions.

The members of a vocation have similar personalities and similar histories of personal development. If a person enters a given vocation because of his particular personality and history, it follows that each vocation attracts and retains people with similar personalities. Laurent's study of engineers, physicians, and lawyers [85] documents the similarities in life history for the members of a vocation. Other studies—by Galinsky [46], Nachmann [97], Roe [105], and Segal [111], for example—lend support to this assumption. And, if we form classes made up of vocations demanding similar personalities, we should get groups of people who are alike. For example, groups of scientists such as physicists, chemists, and mathematicians should be grossly similar, because the evidence indicates that physical scientists have something in common.

Because people in a vocational group have similar personalities, they will respond to many situations and problems in similar ways, and they will create characteristic interpersonal environments. Although we cannot test this assumption directly, we do have some indirect evidence. For example, Astin and Holland [9] were able to predict what college students would say about their college and fellow students. The method entails a simple census of the number of students in each of six curricular groups: Realistic, Intellectual, Social, Conventional, Enterprising, and Artistic. The percentage of students in each curricular group at a given college becomes the profile of that college. In several studies [8, 9], it was found, for example, that the percentage of students in the Realistic group was correlated with a student's description of the college and its students as pragmatic rather than humanistic. It is possible then to describe a college by a simple census of its members, if one has a way to interpret the meaning of membership in various curricula.

Vocational satisfaction, stability, and achievement depend on the congruency between one's personality and the environment (composed largely of other people) in which one works. Just as we are more comfortable among friends whose tastes, talents, and values are similar to ours, so we are more likely to perform well at a vocation in which we "fit" psychologically. The Strong and other generally accepted vocational inventories are based in part on this assumption. Moreover, the vocational literature is filled with evidence that supports the assumption, although that evidence is not usually interpreted as relating to the interaction between a particular personality and a particular environment.

Our knowledge of vocational life is disorganized and often isolated from the main body of psychological and sociological knowledge. At the present time we have a sizable storehouse of vocational knowledge, and like many storehouses, it is a disorganized clutter. We have no comprehensive organizational plans or theories to order this information.

There are literally hundreds of studies that report on such matters as the personal attributes of Coca-Cola bottle workers and the interests of door-to-door salesmen, the vocational inclinations of engineering freshmen, the traits of embalming trainees, and the parental attitudes of scientists. Unfortunately, these studies are only loosely tied together. Generally, there are no maps to help either the professional or the uninitiated. Even with an experienced guide, finding one's way through this jungle is slow and difficult. The area of "vocational interests" is a kind of no man's land in the more settled regions of psychology and sociology.

The origin of our organizational difficulties comes mostly from our neglect of conceptual definitions. Because of our repeated failure to define *interests* conceptually, they have come to mean no more than the scales of the Kuder Preference Record and the Strong Vocational Interest Blank. That is, we have accepted methods of assessment in place of definitions. Our reliance on empirical definitions has cost us much. First, it has led to a vocational interest literature that has only tentative and ambiguous relationships with the mainstreams of social psychology and the psychology of personality. Our studies suggest that interests are related chiefly to other interests or to other interest inventories. And because interest scales have lacked "surplus" meaning, these studies fail to indicate that "interests" are an expression of personality and personal development. The accumulation of many such studies has led to a relatively *independent* literature known as "interest measurement." And, although it has become fashionable in recent years to say that interests are an expression of personality, just saying it doesn't solve the problem, for we have spent more than twenty years acting as if interests and personality were unrelated. Darley and Hagenah [27] recognized the problem when they wrote: "We may have attempted to isolate the individual's occupational life from his total life and life style. We may have given inadequate operational definitions to our terms and concepts. . . . We have been too concerned with the empiric aspects of our problem."

A SUMMARY OF THE THEORY

By regarding interests and vocational preferences as expressions of personality and personal development, we have then a potentially useful model for understanding vocational behavior. The present theory is both a theory of vocational life and a theory of personality. Although it is concerned principally with explaining vocational choice, changes in choice, and vocational achievement, the theory is, to a lesser degree, also concerned with emotional stability, creative performance, and personal development. The construction of a theory of personality from our knowledge of vocational life seems promising, because most vocational behavior is socially valuable and accessible to public examination. In contrast, theories of personality based on sex and family relationships must rely on information that is often private and sensitive to distortion.

The present theory is the outgrowth of a series of empirical and theoretical reports that began with the development of an inventory to measure personality from scales composed of occupational titles [63]. This inventory was followed by "A Theory of Vocational Choice" [64], "A Classification for Occupations in Terms of Personality and Intelligence" [65], and a number of other papers and monographs [8, 9, 67, 68, 69, 70, 71, 72, 110, 118, 35, 43]. All of these studies indicated that it might be useful not only to regard the theory of vocational choice as a theory of personality but also to develop a comprehensive and systematic theory. From this point of view, vocational choice is only one of many expressions of personality. And the way of life associated with a particular occupational class can be regarded as a human environment of which the obvious work activities are only a small part.

The first statement of the theory is perhaps best described as a heuristic theory of personality types and environmental situations [64]. By *heuristic theory* is meant a theory that stimulates research and investigation by its suggestive character rather than

by its logical or systematic structure. The present statement of
the theory makes it more systematic. The theory was written to
organize what we know about vocational behavior and to suggest
some ways for investigating vocational problems and acquiring
new knowledge. Some working definitions have been provided
to facilitate understanding, research, and practical application.

Briefly, the theory consists of several simple ideas and their
more complex elaborations. First, we assume that we can characterize people by their resemblance to one or more personality
types. The closer a person's resemblance to a particular type, the
more likely it is he will exhibit the personal traits and behaviors
associated with that type. Second, we assume that the environments in which people live can be characterized by their resemblance to one or more model environments. Finally, we assume
that the pairing of persons and environments leads to several
outcomes that we can predict and understand from our knowledge of the personality types and the environmental models.
These outcomes include vocational choice, vocational stability
and achievement, personal stability, creative performance, and
susceptibility to influence.

The following statements summarize our major assumptions;
the remaining chapters elaborate these same ideas and indicate
some of the evidence for their validity. These working assumptions constitute the heart of the theory. They indicate the nature
of the personality types, the principles of their determination, and
their relation to various outcomes—achievement, creative performance, and vocational choice.

*In our culture, most persons can be categorized as one of six
types—Realistic, Intellectual, Social, Conventional, Enterprising,
and Artistic.* The description of each type (see Chapter Two) is
both a summary of what we know about people in a given occupational group and a special way of comprehending this
information: a theoretical type. A "type" is a model against
which we can measure the real person. Each type is the product
of a characteristic interaction between a particular heredity and
a variety of cultural and personal forces, including peers, parents,
other significant adults, social class, culture, and the physical

environment. Out of his experience, a person develops habitual ways of coping with the tasks presented by his psychological, social, and physical environment, including vocational situations. His biological and social heredity, coupled with his personal history, creates a characteristic set of abilities, perceptual skills and outlook, life goals, values, self-concepts (his image and evaluation of himself), and coping behavior (his typical methods of dealing with the problems of living). A type is then a complex cluster of personal attributes.

This characteristic cluster creates a number of special predispositions, such as preferences for a particular class of vocations, potentials for various special achievements, and aspirations. For example, if a person resembles the Social type, he would be expected to seek out Social occupations, such as teaching, social work, or the ministry; he would be expected to have socially oriented achievements, such as being elected to school and community positions of leadership; and he would be expected to have socially oriented goals and values—helping others, valuing religion, serving his community.

The present types are analogous in some ways to the types proposed earlier by Adler [1], Fromm [45], Jung [74], Sheldon [112, 113], Spranger [114], and others [34, 80]. They differ from these earlier typologies in their origin—which is largely our vocational literature—and in their definitions (see Chapter Two). The six major factors identified in Guilford's [57] comprehensive factor analysis of human interest—mechanical, scientific, social welfare, clerical, business, and esthetic—approximate the present types. To the best of my knowledge, Guilford's factor analysis is the most explicit forerunner of the present typology.

By comparing a person's attributes with those of each of the model types, we can determine which type he resembles most. That model becomes his "personality type." A person's resemblance to each of the six types yields a pattern of similarity and dissimilarity, the person's personality pattern. Thus, we can obtain a "profile" of resemblances. This method allows for the complexity of personality, thus avoiding some of the problems inherent in categorizing a person as a single type. A six-category scheme assumes that there are only six kinds of people in the world—an unacceptable assumption, even for someone interested in scientific simplicity or numerology. But a six-category scheme that allows a simple ordering of a person's resemblance to *each* of the six models provides the possibility of 720 different personality patterns. If instead of a simple ordering of resemblances we use actual measures of resemblance, then the number of possible personality patterns we can assess becomes much greater still. Consequently, it is possible to use only a few models and yet allow for the complexity of personality. Whether or not such a scheme is also useful is an empirical matter.

To obtain a person's profile, we can use his scores on selected scales from "interest" and personality inventories, his self-descriptions, his choice of vocation or field of training, his life history, or combinations of these data. For example, certain scales of the Vocational Preference Inventory, the Strong Vocational Interest Blank, and the Kuder Preference Record have been designated as estimates of the types. The person's profile can then be interpreted by applying the descriptions of the types.

There are six kinds of environments: Realistic, Intellectual, Social, Conventional, Enterprising, and Artistic. Each environment is dominated by a given type of personality, and each environment is typified by physical settings posing special problems and stresses. For example, Realistic environments are "dominated" by Realistic types of people: that is, the largest percentage of the population in the environment resembles the Realistic type. An Intellectual environment is dominated by Intellectual types; a Social environment by Social types. Where people congregate, they create an environment that reflects the types they are. Thus, the environment can be assessed in the same terms as we assess people individually.

People search for environments and vocations that will permit them to exercise their skills and abilities, to express their attitudes and values, to take on agreeable problems and roles, and to avoid disagreeable ones. Consequently, Realistic types seek Realistic environments, Intellectual types seek Intellectual environments, and so forth. To a lesser degree, environments also search for people through recruiting practices. The person's search for environments is carried on in many ways, at several levels of consciousness, and over a long period of time. The personality types epitomize some common ways in which people develop in our culture. They also illustrate how one's personal development channels one's goals, vocational choices, mobility, and achievement.

Although there have been few studies of the actual process of seeking suitable environments, the study of the antecedents and correlates of vocational choice yields a useful account of the personal and impersonal forces that determine this process. To summarize, as a child grows up, he learns through his parents, social class, schools, and community what he does well, what he does poorly, and what he likes to do. He also acquires some useful though not always accurate vocational images. (It should be pointed out that this knowledge about himself and about different occupations is frequently unconscious.) When he graduates from school and takes his first job, his choice is a resolution of a complex set of forces that include his hierarchy of choices (an outcome of his personality development represented by his personality pattern or "profile"), the range of job opportunities available to him, the influence of parents and friends, and various chance factors. In the present theory, a person's first and subsequent decisions are explained in terms of personality pattern and environmental model only. A more complete theory would incorporate economic and sociological influence.

A person's behavior can be explained by the interaction of his personality pattern and his environment. Put another way, if we know a person's personality pattern and the pattern of his environment, we can, in principle, use our knowledge of personality types and environmental models to forecast some of the outcomes of such a pairing. Such outcomes include choice of training and vocation, level of achievement, creative behavior, personal stability, reaction to stress, sensitivity to particular stresses or threats, occupational mobility, and outstanding accomplishments.

APTITUDE, INTELLIGENCE, AND SEX

Unfortunately most of our empirical knowledge about personality and vocational behavior has been obtained in studies of men. Consequently, it is difficult to construct a theory of personality that applies equally to men and to women. The present theory is no exception: it is based chiefly on studies of men and is probably less useful for understanding the behavior of women. A special but closely related theory for women is desirable, but at this point I have none to offer.

In the present formulations, we have assumed that aptitude and intelligence are less important than personality and interests in determining vocational choice. Further, we have assumed that intelligence and aptitudes are moderately correlated with the various personality types: for example, a person who resembles the Intellectual type is usually intelligent and skilled at abstract reasoning; similarly, people who resemble the Realistic type have mechanical and motor skills. Thus, it seems unnecessary to spell out a series of hypotheses about the role of aptitude and intelligence. A recent study by Mierzwa [95] supports this assumption. In comparing four systems of information for the prediction of vocational choice—interest, environment, temperament, and ability—Mierzwa found that the interest variables proved to be the most accurate predictive system; although other systems added to the predictive accuracy, the gains were small or negligible.

The importance of vocational measures has also been documented by Clark [19]. After several empirical comparisons of the relative efficiency of aptitude and interest inventories, Clark comes to a similar conclusion: ". . . when the problem is one of prediction of occupational choice, or occupational classification, the use of interest measures should receive more consideration than the use of aptitude measures."

SUMMARY

The present chapter outlines the theory of how people make vocational choices. The following chapters are simply a more complete exposition. Chapter Two, "The Personality Types," provides detailed descriptions of the six theoretical types. Chapter Three, "Personality Types and Expected Performance," is an account of some of the ways in which the typology can be used for research and for understanding others. Chapters Four and Five specify "The Environmental Models" and "Environmental Models and Expected Influences," respectively. Chapter Six, "People in Environments," outlines some of the outcomes of the pairing of people and environments. Chapter Seven, "Life Histories," extends the environmental outcomes mentioned in Chapter Six to successive person–environment interactions over long periods of time—the life history. Chapter Eight, "Research and Practical Applications," suggests some of the research problems and the potential applications of the theory.

CHAPTER TWO

The Personality Types

THE FORMULATIONS for the types grew out of my experience as a vocational counselor and a clinician and out of my construction of a personality inventory from interest materials. After reviewing the vocational literature—especially factor analytic studies of personality and vocational interests—I concluded that it might be useful to categorize people into six types: Realistic, Intellectual, Social, Conventional, Enterprising, and Artistic.

This clinical interpretation of the interest and personality literature and its annual revisions were developed over a ten-year period. Primarily, it was a persistent attempt to find a way to summarize and comprehend the vast array of evidence about the nature of personality and interest. The idea for a typology resulted from my frequent observation that several broad classes account for most so-called "independent" human interests, traits, and behavior. Later as I began to organize the literature into categories, bits and pieces of the evidence for a major category suggested fragmentary stereotypes. A now obscure article by Darley [26] in 1938 had suggested the potential value of organizing our knowledge in terms of occupational stereotypes. The typologies based on physique, temperament, and personality reinforced my interest in this orientation. Continued review and collection of new evidence strengthened my belief in the validity of these ideas and in the value of an explicit and thorough typology.

DESCRIPTIONS OF THE TYPES

The types are assumed to represent common outcomes of growing up in our culture. Each type is described in terms of a theoretical model called the *model orientation*. The model orientation is a cluster of characteristic adaptive behaviors (coping mechanisms), psychological needs and motives, self-concepts, life history, vocational and educational goals, preferred occupational roles, aptitudes, and intelligence. A person's resemblance to *each* of the six model orientations is called his *personality pattern*. The single model that the person most closely resembles is his *personality type*.

TABLE 1

The Personality Types and the Vocational Preferences Defining Each Type

REALISTIC. The model type is masculine, physically strong, unsociable, aggressive; has good motor coordination and skill; lacks verbal and interpersonal skills; prefers concrete to abstract problems; conceives of himself as being aggressive and masculine and as having conventional political and economic values. Persons who choose or prefer the following occupations resemble this type: airplane mechanic, construction inspector, electrician, filling station attendant, fish and wildlife specialist, locomotive engineer, master plumber, photoengraver, power shovel operator, power station operator, radio operator, surveyor, tree surgeon, tool designer.

INTELLECTUAL. The model type is task-oriented, intraceptive, asocial; prefers to think through rather than act out problems; needs to understand; enjoys ambiguous work tasks; has unconventional values and attitudes; is anal as opposed to oral. Vocational preferences include aeronautical design engineer, anthropologist, astronomer, biologist, botanist, chemist, editor of a scientific journal, geologist, independent research scientist, meteorologist, physicist, scientific research worker, writer of scientific or technical articles, zoologist.

SOCIAL. The model type is sociable, responsible, feminine, humanistic, religious; needs attention; has verbal and interpersonal skills; avoids

TABLE 1—*Continued*

intellectual problem solving, physical activity, and highly ordered activities; prefers to solve problems through feelings and interpersonal manipulations of others; is orally dependent. Vocational preferences include assistant city school superintendent, clinical psychologist, director of welfare agency, foreign missionary, high school teacher, juvenile delinquency expert, marriage counselor, personal counselor, physical education teacher, playground director, psychiatric case worker, social science teacher, speech therapist, vocational counselor.

CONVENTIONAL. The model type prefers structured verbal and numerical activities and subordinate roles; is conforming (extraceptive); avoids ambiguous situations and problems involving interpersonal relationships and physical skills; is effective at well-structured tasks; identifies with power; values material possessions and status. Vocational preferences include: bank examiner, bank teller, bookkeeper, budget reviewer, cost estimator, court stenographer, financial analyst, IBM equipment operator, inventory controller, payroll clerk, quality control expert, statistician, tax expert, traffic manager.

ENTERPRISING. The model type has verbal skills for selling, dominating, leading; conceives of himself as a strong, masculine leader; avoids well-defined language or work situations requiring long periods of intellectual effort; is extraceptive; differs from the Conventional type in that he prefers ambiguous social tasks and has a greater concern with power, status, and leadership; is orally aggressive. Vocational preferences include business executive, buyer, hotel manager, industrial relations consultant, manufacturer's representative, master of ceremonies, political campaign manager, real-estate salesman, restaurant worker, speculator, sports promoter, stock and bond salesman, television producer, traveling salesman.

ARTISTIC. The model type is asocial; avoids problems that are highly structured or require gross physical skills; resembles the Intellectual type in being intraceptive and asocial; but differs from that type in that he has a need for individualistic expression, has less ego strength, is more feminine, and suffers more frequently from emotional disturbances; prefers dealing with environmental problems through self-expression in artistic media. Vocational preferences include art dealer, author, cartoonist, commercial artist, composer, concert singer, dramatic coach, free-lance writer, musical arranger, musician, playwright, poet, stage director, symphony conductor.

The description of each type consists of an empirical summary and a theoretical formulation. The empirical summaries were derived by using lists of occupational titles (see Table 1). Information about persons employed in or having preferences for, or "interests" in, different occupations was categorized by these criteria. In this way, a large portion of the voluminous vocational literature was sorted into six conceptual bins so that it could be comprehended with greater ease. Thus it was possible to check for empirical consistencies or inconsistencies as well as to test the theoretical value of such a classification.

The information for the empirical summaries comes from diverse sources: several reports on the vocational choices of high-aptitude students [67, 68, 69, 72], a summary of the relationships between "vocational interests" and personality variables abstracted from fifteen correlational studies [65], a reorganization of the empirical information in the book *Ten Thousand Careers* [128], to name a few.* All findings reported in the empirical summaries are statistically significant.

Such a classification introduces error, because we have integrated information obtained from groups of students and adults who differ in age, education, and aptitude. To reduce error, the empirical model incorporates only those results that are found in at least two different studies. (Because it is based on a very large sample, the information from *Ten Thousand Careers* is an exception to this rule.) In addition, only those personal attributes that discriminate most efficiently across the six types are retained. For a more explicit account of these discriminations the reader should consult the full reports cited earlier.

The preparation of the empirical summaries provided a means for looking at some of our knowledge about vocational behavior and personality in a special way—a typology of six model personalities. The empirical portions of the summaries that follow are consistent with the literature of vocational behavior. In fact,

---

* For other sources see references numbered 15, 21, 25, 26, 27, 28, 32, 41, 44, 46, 47, 48, 49, 53, 54, 57, 60, 71, 79, 82, 97, 98, 101, 103, 105, 107, 111, 116, 123, 130, 131, and 140.

at the time these studies were done, all the information available on the same variable for each of the six types was used. Obviously, information about people of one or two types is of little value, because it does not tell us how the assessed types compare with the excluded types. Additional empirical study is required before we will be able to rely on the specific validity of each item in these empirical summaries;[*] however, our practice was to derive what meaning we could from such information by assuming its validity; had we assumed that this method of classification simply confounded error, any interpretation would have been meaningless.

The *theoretical* formulations for each type are assumed to be consistent with their empirical summaries, but they were arrived at by a subjective process. They should be regarded as potentially useful speculations rather than as substantive accounts of our knowledge.

The description of each type is organized as follows: conceptual and empirical definitions, personality (empirical summary), personality (theoretical formulation). Criteria for distinguishing between models having common characteristics are also included.

The Realistic Model

Conceptual Definition. The Realistic person copes with his physical and social environment by selecting goals, values, and tasks that entail the objective, concrete valuation and manipulation of things, tools, animals, and machines; and by avoiding goals, values, and tasks that require subjectivity, intellectualism, artistic expression, and social sensitivity and skill. The Realistic type is masculine, unsociable, emotionally stable, materialistic, genuine, concretistic, and oriented to the present.

[*] For an exhaustive review of the vocational literature it is necessary to consult many textbooks, review articles, and journals. Such a review will turn up some evidence that contradicts the summaries for each type, but these contradictions do not, I think, seriously impair the main findings in the present empirical summaries.

Empirical Definition. The Realistic person prefers, is training for, or works at such occupations as the following:

Master plumber	Weather observer
Photographer	Radio operator
Machinist	Electronic technician
Hunter-trapper	Electrician
Power station operator	House painter
Aviator	Crane operator
Construction inspector	Photoengraver
Army officer	Locomotive engineer
Surveyor	Tree surgeon
Tool designer	Carpenter
Fish and wildlife specialist	Filling station attendant
Truck driver	Ranch hand (cowboy)
Automobile mechanic	Draftsman
Forest ranger	Airplane mechanic
Power shovel operator	

Personality (Empirical Summary). The following sections characterize the Realistic person in terms of the evidence from the research literature.

Goals and Values: Prefers agricultural, technical, skilled trade, and engineering vocations. Has conventional values, especially economic values. Holds that esthetic values are of little importance.

Identifications and Preferred Roles: Admires Admiral Byrd and Thomas Edison; likes athletic, masculine, unsociable, natural member or participant roles; avoids supervisory and leadership roles.

Preferred Activities: Likes activities that involve motor skills, things, realism, structure. Such activities include athletics, scouting, crafts, science projects, collecting, mechanical drawing, shopwork, mechanics, marksmanship, racing, gardening.

Aversions: Avoids social situations requiring independent self-expression (personalized and artistic roles), where he would be the center of attention; avoids intellectual and verbal tasks that require abstract thinking and reading; avoids work situations that emphasize proper dress, conventional manners and speech, and socially acceptable personality traits.

Self-Concept: Sees himself as mature, masculine, practical, conventional, persistent, unsociable, abasing, submissive, natural (not exhibitionistic), favorable to change, and having a narrow range of interests. Rates himself low in self-confidence, writing, speaking, originality, and leadership.

Achievement and Originality: Achieves primarily in technical and athletic areas; tends to do poorly in academic, social, and artistic areas. The Realistic type is one of two least original of the six types: he rarely performs creatively.

Outlook and Perception: Has simple rather than complex outlook; is dependent upon others rather than independent in judgment; on objective tests, his perceptual skills show a constrictive quality and an inability to integrate diverse stimuli.

Aptitudes and Special Abilities: Has more mathematical than verbal aptitude; his mechanical and psychomotor skills exceed his numerical, verbal, and perceptual aptitudes.

Personality (Theoretical Formulation). The Realistic person asserts himself by developing athletic and motor skills, by identifying with physical heroes and practical men, and by acquiring material possessions. The operation of machines, tools, and vehicles (especially large or powerful ones) serves to increase his sense of well-being and power.

He reduces stress by limiting his social relationships, by avoiding intellectual or introverted tasks and activities, by avoiding new tasks, and by playing masculine roles. He defends himself in social relationships by playing a passive or submissive role, by being self-abasing, and by developing his physical skills as compensation for his lack of intellectual and social skills.

The Realistic person differs from the Intellectual person in that the Realistic person is more practical (concerned with facts), emotionally stable, masculine, and conventional (more concerned about success, status, and leadership) than the Intellectual person. The Realistic person is less scholarly (less apt to seek a Ph.D. or daydream about achievement and learning), original, sociable, insightful about interpersonal relations, independent, and self-confident than the Intellectual person. The Realistic person differs from the Social and the Enterprising person primarily in social skills and interests. The Realistic person is more masculine and less original than the Artistic person. The Realistic person differs from the Conventional person primarily in that the Realistic person is less responsible and sociable and more impulsive, stable, masculine, submissive, and self-deprecatory.

Background and Personal Development. A particular type of background and developmental history produces a particular type of personality, although our evidence on exact relationships is grossly incomplete. The mother and father of the Realistic type tend to be poorly educated and are often foreign-born. The facilities in his home—many tools but few books—provide a special experience that is conducive to the outcome associated with this type. The lower socioeconomic status of the family is consistent with the self-abasement of the Realistic type. This abasement may occur in part because of a failure to acquire a useful range of social and personal competencies in the process of growing up, because families of lower socioeconomic status are less able to provide training, equipment, and personal time for such purposes.

Generally, the role of parental attitudes in vocational choice is unclear. Although a few positive results have occurred, the relationships between parental attitudes and vocational choices for this type have been very small and often negligible [55, 67, 117, 133].

The Intellectual Model

Conceptual Definition. The Intellectual person copes with the social and physical environment through the use of intelligence: he solves problems primarily through the manipulation of ideas, words, and symbols rather than through his physical and social skills.

The Intellectual person is characterized by such adjectives as analytical, rational, independent, radical, abstract, introverted, anal, cognitive, critical, curious, and perceptive.

Empirical Definition. The Intellectual person prefers, is training for, or works in such occupations as the following:

Physicist	Writer of scientific or technical
Surgeon	articles
Scientific research worker	Editor of scientific journal
Botanist	Geologist
Experimental psychologist	Veterinarian
Interplanetary scientist	Architect
Astronomer	Scientific authority
Inventor	Archeologist
Aeronautical design engineer	Science-fiction writer
Anthropologist	Meteorologist
Zoologist	Biologist
Atomic scientist	Scientific theorist
Chemist	Experimental laboratory
Independent research scientist	engineer
Mathematician	

Personality (Empirical Summary). The following sections characterize the Intellectual person in terms of the empirical evidence.

Goals and Values: Prefers scientific vocations; values theoretical and, to a lesser degree, esthetic problems and tasks.

Identifications and Preferred Roles: Admires Curie, Darwin, Russell, Oppenheimer, and Burbank; prefers the role of an independent worker, neither giving nor receiving any support; prefers to be himself (not an actor).

Preferred Activities: Likes activities through which he can express his asocial, analytic, imaginative orientation: reading, scientific projects, collecting, scouting, photography, algebra, foreign languages, physics, trigonometry, and such creative activities as art, music, and sculpture.

Aversions and Threats: Avoids situations requiring social skills or aggressive and difficult social interactions.

Self-Concept: Sees himself as unsociable, masculine, persistent, self-controlled, independent, scholarly, intellectual, introverted, submissive, abasing, original, not exhibitionistic, not nurturant or succorant, unpopular, and achieving.

Achievement and Originality: Achieves primarily in academic

and scientific areas. Tends to do poorly as a leader. The Intellectual type is one of two most original of the six types. He obtains high scores on originality scales and tends to win awards, prizes, and recognition for creative accomplishments in science.

Outlook and Perception: Has a complex rather than simple outlook, good spatial reorganizational abilities, and flexible readjustment of adaptation level. Is relatively uninfluenced by tilted frame (tachistoscopic experiments). These qualities imply independence and originality [25].

Aptitudes and Special Abilities: Scores high in both verbal and mathematical aptitudes.

Personal Development: Our knowledge of the family background is limited. Father and mother tend to be well educated, relative to parents of other types. Fathers express approval of son's curiosity and mothers appear to have permissive attitudes about child training.

Personality (Theoretical Formulations). The Intellectual person asserts himself by gaining power through knowledge and intellectual achievement. This maneuver frequently leads to extensive though indirect control over other persons. His intellectuality is probably in part a compensation for lack of social and motor skills; it may be the result of the direct approval of his intelligence and its potential by his well-educated parents.

He reduces stresses by avoiding others (insularity), projecting (defensive hostility), rationalizing (intellectualization), and obtaining safety through knowledge (perfectionism, unassailability). Similarly, he defends himself in social situations by being submissive, self-abasing, and, when pressed, negative. His self-abasement may have its origin in the discrepancy between his idealized image of what he should be and the reality of what he is. (In contrast, the Realistic person's abasement is probably the result of inadequate training because of his low socioeconomic origins.)

The differences between the Intellectual person and the Realistic person were summarized previously (see definition of the Realistic person). The Intellectual person differs from the Artistic person in that the Artistic person is more feminine, impulsive, irresponsible, and unstable, and makes greater use of his feelings and intuitions as guides to problem solving and creating works of art. The Intellectual person is less sociable and conventional than the Social, Conventional, and Enterprising persons.

The Social Model

Conceptual Definition. The Social person copes with his environment by selecting goals, values, and tasks in which he can use his skills with an interest in other persons in order to train or change their behavior. The Social person is typified by his social skills and his need for social interaction; his characteristics include sociability, nurturance, social presence, capacity for status, dominance, and psychological-mindedness. He is concerned with the welfare of dependent persons: the poor, uneducated, sick, unstable, young, and aged. In problem solving, he relies on his emotions and feelings rather than on his intellectual resources.

Empirical Definition. The Social person prefers, is training for, or works at such occupations as the following:

World peace organizer	Elementary-school teacher
Psychiatric case worker	YMCA secretary
Personal counselor	Truant officer (education)
Assistant city school superintendent	Clinical psychologist
	Playground director
Conciliator (employer-employee)	School principal
	Physical education teacher
Judge	Marriage counselor
Psychiatrist	Speech therapist
Juvenile delinquency expert	Director of welfare agency
High school teacher	Public health officer
Foreign missionary	Pediatrician
Employment interviewer	Public relations man
Boy scout official	Social worker
Social science teacher	Vocational counselor

Personality (Empirical Summary). The following sections characterize the Social person in terms of the empirical evidence.

Goals and Values: Prefers educational, therapeutic, and religious vocations. Values social, ethical, and religious activities and problems.

Identifications and Preferred Roles: Prefers activities involving religious, social, and esthetic expression, including church, student government, community services, music, reading, sports, writing, dramatics, public speaking, foreign languages, history, arranging entertainment, journalism, and creative hobbies in art, music, and literature.

Aversions and Threats: Avoids masculine roles that require motor skills, use of tools and machines, or physical danger. Such activities include shopwork, horsemanship, racing, auto repair, model building.

Self-Concept: Sees himself as sociable, nurturant, cheerful, adventurous, effeminate, conservative, dependent, dominant, not scholarly, responsible (superego), psychological-minded, intellectually efficient, achieving, self-accepting, impulsive, not succorant. Rates himself high on leadership, speaking skills, popularity, originality, drive to achieve, dependability, scholarship, aggressiveness, self-control, conservatism, practical-mindedness, expressiveness, self-understanding, perseverance. Has a positive self-image.

Achievement and Originality: Of the six types, he ranks about third on potential for original behavior. His achievements tend to be in the areas of leadership, art, and scholarship (good grades).

Outlook and Perception: On objective (mostly tachistoscopic) measurements or tests, he has flexible readjustment of adaptation level (associated with originality), is influenced by tilted frame (associated with dependence and identification with others), is not affected by "position influence" (associated with lack of constriction), and has poor reorganizational abilities [25].

Aptitudes and Special Abilities: Tends to have high verbal but low mathematical aptitude.

Personal Development: The Social type frequently comes from a rural area. Adolescents with rural backgrounds appear to be more responsible, less antagonistic toward parents and other authorities, and more perfectionistic and paranoid than are adolescents from urban backgrounds. These adolescent characteristics are consonant with the attributes of the adult Social type [60].

Father and mother are well educated relative to other types: they tend to have many books in the home. Fathers seem to place a high value on self-control and a low value on curiosity; this finding is consistent with the Social person's problem-solving style.

Personality (Theoretical Formulation). The Social person asserts and enhances himself by helping dependent persons (the weak, young, and sick) and by concerning himself with human welfare. In this way he gains love, recognition, and status, both social and vocational. His need for cordial personal relationships are conscious, but his needs for dependency, admiration, power, and prestige are usually unconscious.

The Social person diminishes stress and anxiety by repression and denial, and by choosing vocations where the social roles are well-defined: doctor-patient, teacher-student, supervisor-subordinate, minister-congregation. He also deals with stress and anxiety by playing a dependent, ingratiating role with others, by not deferring gratification of bodily urges (food and sex), by controlling others, and by moving toward other persons.

The Social person differs from the Enterprising person in being more feminine, introverted, helpful, intellectual, insightful, cooperative, friendly, responsible (having religious and social values), and less energetic, aggressive, dominant, sociable, adventurous, cynical, and enthusiastic. The Social person differs from the Conventional person in that the latter is more self-controlled, hard-headed, masculine, and submissive. The Social person is more sociable, dependent, and conventional than the Artistic person.

The Conventional Model

Conceptual Definition. The Conventional person copes with his physical and social environment by selecting goals, tasks, and values that are sanctioned by custom and society. Accordingly, his approach to problems is stereotyped, practical, correct; it lacks spontaneity and originality. His personal traits are consistent with this orientation. He is well-controlled, neat, sociable, and creates a good impression. He is somewhat inflexible, conservative, and persevering.

Empirical Definition. The Conventional person prefers, is training for, or works at such occupations as the following:

Bank teller	Efficiency expert
Court stenographer	Insurance clerk
IBM equipment operator	Budget reviewer
Tax expert	Quality control expert
Cashier	Bookkeeper
Administrative secretary	Certified public accountant
Statistician	Bank examiner
Payroll clerk	Records supervisor
Real-estate appraiser	Cost estimator
Post office clerk	Shipping and receiving clerk
Financial analyst	Banker
Inventory controller	Office manager
Traffic manager	Administrative assistant
Credit investigator	Chief clerk

Personality (Empirical Summary). The following sections characterize the Conventional person in terms of the empirical evidence.

Goals and Values: Prefers clerical and computational tasks; places a high value on economic matters and a low value on esthetic and religious matters.

Identifications and Preferred Roles: Identifies with businessmen, especially financial giants: Baruch, Ford, Morgan, Wanamaker, etc. His role preferences are unclear. Some evidence suggests both a preference for subordinate supervisory roles and a desire to act as expert or consultant.

Preferred Activities: His likes suggest a desire for passive and often structured activity: dramatics, music, school journalism, collecting, economics, arithmetic, spelling, typing.

Aversions: Avoids or dislikes common aggressive, masculine

outlets or tasks that require spontaneous, original, integrative functioning. Such activities include shopwork and mechanical drawing, auto repair, diving, marksmanship, sailing, racing, boxing, football, writing technical reports, essays, or poems.

Self-Concept: Sees himself as masculine (a defense?), shrewd, conservative, dominant, playful (not deferring gratification), subject to parental press for achievement, conscientious, sociable, underachieving (academically), controlled, rigid, dependent, intellectually inefficient, making a good impression, stable, self-accepting. Rates himself low as a leader but high on dependability, scholarship, neatness, conservatism, practical-mindedness, cheerfulness, and perseverance. Rated low by others on speaking skills and leadership.

Achievement and Originality: Relative to the other types, the Conventional person is one of the two types with the least potential for creative performance. This outcome is extremely consistent with our current knowledge of creativity and of this type [92, 93].

Outlook and Perception: On tachistoscopic tests, he is inflexible in readjustment of adaptation level (stereotyped and unoriginal), subject to position influence (constricted), and unable to reorganize well. Originality scales imply that he has a simple rather than a complex outlook and that he is dependent upon others in his judgments [25].

Aptitudes and Special Abilities: Has more mathematical than verbal aptitude.

Personal Development: The correlation between family background and adult personality is closer for the Conventional type than for any of the other types. The father places a low value on being curious and independent. The mother, who tends to be a somewhat isolated person, expresses restrictive attitudes about child training; she suppresses sex and aggression. She encourages action rather than reading or intellectual concerns. Although this evidence comes from a grossly atypical sample, it seems clearly and psychologically consistent with the passive, unoriginal, constricted attributes of the Conventional person.

Personality (Theoretical Formulation). The Conventional person enhances himself by identifying with great financial and business leaders, by acquiring possessions, and by playing the role of the good subordinate. He denies his dependency and emphasizes the importance of perfection, prestige, and ambition. Through this coping behavior he gains social and vocational status.

The Conventional person lessens stress and anxiety by conforming to cultural norms and values and by identifying himself with them. Likewise, he attains comfort by ingratiating himself with others and by limiting his social relationships to people he knows well. By avoiding persuasive and expressive activities, he avoids dealing with his own and other people's feelings—phenomena he cannot cope with easily because of his repressive early training. Similarly, he defends himself by maintaining self-control, being dependent, dealing with externals, repressing and denying, rigidly restricting his life within narrow boundaries, and limiting his involvement with his work and with other people. His choice of rule-oriented vocations, with their explicit standards of right and wrong, expresses his life style succinctly.

The Conventional person is most closely related to the Enterprising and the Social person. He differs from the Enterprising person in being less sociable, aggressive, dominant, original, enthusiastic (surgent), impulsive, self-confident, and adventurous. He is also more responsible, dependent, and conservative than the Enterprising person. The Conventional person differs from the Social person in that he possesses greater self-control, is more hard-headed, and is less dominant and nurturant.

The Enterprising Model

Conceptual Definition. The Enterprising person copes with his world by selecting goals, values, and tasks through which he can express his adventurous, dominant, enthusiastic, energetic, and impulsive qualities. The Enterprising person is characterized also by his persuasive, verbal, extroverted, self-accepting, self-confident, oral aggressive, exhibitionistic attributes.

Empirical Definition. The Enterprising person prefers, is training for, or works at such occupations as the following:

Car salesman	Restaurant manager
Personnel manager	President of manufacturing
Liquor salesman	company
Congressional lobbyist	Business executive
Buyer	Television producer
Manufacturer's representative	Industrial relations man
Sales engineer	Business promoter
Amusement park manager	Speculator
Real-estate salesman	Life insurance salesman
Sales manager	Route salesman
Traveling salesman	Radio program director
Auctioneer	Stock and bond salesman
Master of ceremonies	Political campaign manager
Politician	Travel consultant
Hotel manager	Sports promoter
Insurance manager	

Personality (Empirical Summary). The following sections characterize the Enterprising person in terms of the empirical evidence.

Goals and Values: Prefers sales, supervisory, and leadership vocations; places a high value on political and economic matters and a low value on theoretical and esthetic matters.

Identifications and Preferred Roles: Admires Carnegie, Churchill, Ford, Wanamaker; likes masculine, powerful, leadership roles, usually in an expensive setting.

Preferred Activities: Prefers social roles and activities in which he can gratify his needs for dominance, artistic and verbal expression, and recognition, and in which he can play masculine, persuasive, or powerful roles. Such activities include athletics, dramatics, writing, economics, English, foreign language, music, public speaking, baseball, boxing, rowing, tennis, racing, swimming, selling, writing technical reports, arranging entertainment, writing essays or poems, interviewing, soliciting for charity, journalism, amateur motion pictures. The Enterprising type engages in more activities than any other type.

Aversions: Dislikes confining, manual, nonsocial activities—for example, crafts, shopwork, and auto mechanics—or academic activities requiring persistence and extended concentration.

Self-Concept: Sees himself as dominant, sociable, cheerful, adventurous, conservative, impulsive, not scholarly, playful (does not defer gratification frequently), subject to parental controls, not intellectual, self-accepting (high positive self-evaluation), stable, and desiring high status. Rates himself high on speaking skills and leadership, emotional stability, popularity, athletic ability, aggressiveness, practical-mindedness, cheerfulness, and self-confidence.

Achievement and Originality: Achieves in athletics and in persuasive (leadership) and, to a lesser extent, artistic areas. Relative to other types, his potential for original behavior is about average.

Outlook and Perception: On tachistoscopic tasks the Enterprising person has poor reorganizational ability. His outlook is colored by intense political convictions and status-oriented values.

Personal Development: The Enterprising person comes from an urban rather than a rural area. His parents have a high socioeconomic status and are well educated; they have many books in the home. His mother has pushed his development and suppressed his interest in sex: these attitudes are conducive to some of his adult attributes. His father wants him to be popular rather than curious.

This background appears to reinforce the Enterprising person's needs for recognition, love, and material rewards, which he seeks in vocations providing similar gratifications. Such a background helps to explain why the Enterprising person avoids academic and intellectual vocations and moves toward people.

Personality (Theoretical Formulation). The Enterprising person asserts and enhances himself by struggling for power and control, by developing his athletic abilities, by acquiring possessions, and by exploiting others. Some of these activities lead to the acquisition of social and vocational status.

He lessens stress and anxiety through hyperactivity, drinking and eating, sexual expression, wit and humor, and repression and denial. His defenses include oral aggression, dependence on others, narcissism, regression, self-aggrandizement, identification with strong leaders, and rationalization.

The Enterprising person differs from the Artistic person in that the latter is more introverted, feminine, self-deprecating, creative, unstable, independent, unconventional, and unsociable.

The Artistic Model

Conceptual Definition. The Artistic person copes with his physical and social environment by using his feelings, emotions, intuitions, and imagination to create art forms or products. For the Artistic person, problem solving involves expressing his imagination and taste through the conception and execution of his art.

Similarly, he relies principally on his subjective impressions and fantasies for interpretations of and solutions to environmental problems. The Artistic person is characterized further by his complexity of outlook, independence of judgment, introversion, and originality.

Empirical Definition. The Artistic person prefers, is training for, or works at such occupations as the following:

Furniture designer	Musical arranger
Translator	Art dealer
Humorist	Window decorator
Art critic	Newspaper reporter
Stage designer	Sculptor
Poet	Interior decorator
Novelist	Music critic
Symphony conductor	Clothing designer
Musician	Composer
Dance band leader	Stage director
Commercial artist	Playwright
Actor	Cartoonist
Free-lance writer	Concert singer
Portrait artist	Dramatic coach

Personality (Empirical Summary). The following sections characterize the Artistic person in terms of the empirical evidence.

Goals and Values: Prefers musical, artistic, literary, and dramatic vocations. Values esthetics, and places little importance on political and economic matters.

Identifications and Preferred Roles: Identifies with famous artists and intellectuals: Caruso, Picasso, Eliot, and Russell. Wants to be an independent, creative artist. More typically, he tends to become a teacher in his artistic specialty.

Preferred Activities: Prefers hobbies and activities of a somewhat creative character: debating, music, school journalism, student government, community service, collecting, photography, English, history, arranging entertainment, writing poems or essays, painting, creative writing.

Aversions: Dislikes masculine activities and roles—auto repair, athletics.

Self-Concept: Sees himself as unsociable, feminine, submissive, introspective, depressive, abasing, sensitive (paranoid), independent, radical, impulsive, flexible, irresponsible, achieving, unstable, naïve, tense, and subject to parental press for achievement. Rates himself high on writing skills, originality, neatness, independence, expressiveness, and self-confidence but low on popularity.

Achievement and Originality: Achieves primarily in artistic fields. On originality measures, he generally has higher scores than any other type. Creative performance in the arts exceeds that of all other types.

Outlook and Perception: On objective tachistoscopic tests, he is not influenced by tilted frame (independence). Has complex, flexible, independent, unconventional outlook [25].

Aptitudes and Special Abilities: Verbal aptitudes usually greatly exceed mathematical aptitudes. Has exceptional perceptual and motor skills that are conducive to excellence in the arts.

Personal Development: The relationship between the Artistic person's family background and his adult characteristics is not clear. His mother expresses equalitarian attitudes about child training; his father hopes his children will be self-controlled and is less concerned with their ability to defend themselves or their dependability. The Artistic person comes from an above-average socioeconomic group.

Personality (Theoretical Formulation). By expressing and developing his artistic talent, the Artistic person asserts himself in a socially acceptable manner and thus gains approval and recognition. Simultaneously, he has learned to relate to people through the indirect medium of his art and thus to compensate for his estrangement from others.

To find relief from anxiety and the stresses of interpersonal relationships, he avoids numerous direct relationships with others. His rejection of conventional values is a part of his movement away from others. This rejection is advantageous to him, because by being included in but not intimately involved with the culture, he is relatively free to think, imagine, and create new forms without being as bound by cultural values as most people are.

His self-sufficiency also springs from his lack of attachment to others. Likewise, his perfectionistic trends are in part attempts to acquire an unassailability, although such trends are also the outgrowth of his having adopted strong ego ideals at an early age. These high ideals may lead to abasement because of the disparity between his ideals and his accomplishments. In their extreme forms, his detachment, asociability, and rejection of cultural values becomes negativism. The productive artist probably falls between the extremes of unquestioning acceptance and total rejection of the culture.

The Artistic person defends himself also by projection, a natural outcome of his failure to maintain the corrective communication that good interpersonal relationships provide. His lack of socialization permits him to use his primitive and childish impulses in his particular medium. Unfortunately, this lack also makes him more likely to develop regressive disorders.

ASSESSMENT OF TYPES

The empirical definitions of the types make it possible to examine the validity of the descriptions and to use the typology in working with adolescents and adults. Several related methods have been used to assess a person's resemblance to these types.

We can assess a person's personality type by *qualitative* methods: a person may express vocational preferences and interests or hold employment in an occupation that is characteristic of a type; he may express preferences for or be engaged in educational training that is characteristic of a type. For example, he may want to become a physicist, be employed as a physicist, plan to major in physics, or be enrolled as a physics major; any one of these four kinds of information results in his being classified as an Intellectual type. This classification is accomplished by comparing his educational or vocational interests with vocations assumed to be typical of each personality type (Table 1 contains these vocational criteria). In the preceding example, "physicist" is one of the occupations that define the Intellectual type. To take another example, a teacher would be classified as a Social type, because "teacher" is one of the vocational criteria of this type. The use of this simple qualitative procedure in research, although helpful, made clear the need for a more accurate method of assessment.

Various quantitative methods have also been used to assess a person's resemblance to the types. The Realistic, Intellectual, Social, Conventional, Enterprising, and Artistic scales of the Vocational Preference Inventory [62] provide a simple, brief procedure for typing a person. First, the subject indicates the vocations that appeal to him and those that do not from a list of 84 occupational titles [14 occupations for each of the six scales]. The six scales are scored and profiled. The higher a person's score on a scale, the greater his resemblance to the type that scale represents. His highest score represents his *dominant personality type*; his profile of scores (obtained by ranking

TABLE 2

Personality Types and Their Definitions

Definition	1 Realistic	2 Intellectual	3 Social	4 Conventional	5 Enterprising	6 Artistic
Vocational Preference Inventory (VPI) Scale Scores	Realistic	Intellectual	Social	Conventional	Enterprising	Artistic
Strong Scale Scores (SVIB)	Aviator (Gp. IV)	Physicist (Gps. I–II)	Social Science Teacher (Gp. V)	Accountant (Gps. VII–VIII)	Sales Manager (Gp. IX)	Artist, Musician, Author-Journalist
Kuder Preference Scales	Outdoor, Mechanical	Scientific	Social Service	Computational, Clerical	Persuasive	Artistic, Musical, Literary
Choice of Major Field*	Engineering, Agriculture	Physics, Math	Education, Social Science	Accounting, Economics	Business Administration, Political Scientist	Art, Music
Choice of Vocation*	Surveyor, Mechanic	Chemist, Physicist	Teacher, Vocational Counselor	Accountant, Clerk	Salesman, Executive	Artist, Writer
Current Occupation Work History	Realistic →	Intellectual →	Social →	Conventional →	Enterprising →	Artistic →
Personal Survey Scores						

NOTE: For example, persons with high scores on any of the following scales are assumed to resemble the Realistic personality type: Realistic scale (Vocational Preference Inventory); Aviator scale and remaining Group IV scales (Strong Vocational Interest Blank); Outdoor and Mechanical scales (Kuder Preference Record); Realistic scale (Personal Survey); choices of major fields such as agriculture and engineering and of occupations such as mechanic, farmer, or engineer.

* See Appendix A for a more complete list of the major fields and occupations defining each type.

the scale scores from highest to lowest) represents his *personality pattern*.

The Strong Vocational Interest Blank [121] has also been used to assess a person's resemblance to each type. For example, the Aviator scale of the Strong was used to represent the Realistic type, the Physicist scale to represent the Intellectual type, the Social Science Teacher scale for the Social type, the Accountant scale for the Conventional type, the Sales Manager scale for the Enterprising type, and the Musician scale for the Artistic type. In principle, the Kuder Preference Record [84] and other interest inventories can also be used for this purpose.

The Personal Survey (see Appendix B), a brief experimental inventory, was designed for the express purpose of defining a person's type. To develop the inventory, items that best discriminated among types were selected from several studies [67, 68, 69, 72]. They were chosen with the view of obtaining a comprehensive assessment of the subject's goals and values, self-concepts, competencies, coping behavior, identifications, and interests. For each kind of content, there are an equal number of items. The survey includes, among other things, a list of self-descriptive adjectives (for example, *aloof, argumentative, introverted*), self-ratings of other traits and abilities (*absent-mindedness, mechanical ability, originality*), ratings of the relative importance of various life goals, and ratings of famous people thought worthy of emulation. The Personal Survey may in the future provide more useful definitions and better predictions than the Vocational Preference Inventory or the Strong Vocational Interest Blank. Table 2 summarizes the qualitative and quantitative methods for defining the types.

In short, we have defined a person's resemblance to each type by his vocational interests as manifested in his vocational and educational preferences, his current employment, or his scores on certain interest scales. These definitions are "approximate," because they are working definitions whose simplicity lends itself to research and redefinition. At present, the Vocational Preference Inventory is probably the most satisfactory assessment method for several reasons. First, the VPI scales have been studied most extensively for this purpose. Second, these scales

are equal in length and have useful homogeneity, ranging from
.76 to .85 (K–R 20). Finally, because the scales are composed
only of occupational titles, they make it easy to coordinate
several similar definitions of each of the six types. That is, the
lists of occupations defining the types were used not only to
designate various educational and vocational choices as being
characteristic of a type but also to indicate the vocational interest inventory scales that should be used to assess resemblance
to a type. For example, the Aviator scale of the Strong Vocational
Interest Blank was used as a measure of the Realistic type, because "aviator" is among the occupations comprising the list of
Realistic occupations. Similarly, the Scientific scale of the Kuder
Preference Record is assumed to be a measure of a person's
Intellectual orientation, because the Intellectual list is comprised
of scientific vocations. In addition, academic major fields closely
associated with the occupations defining each type have been
classified accordingly.

The different definitions for a given type in Table 2 are assumed to be positively intercorrelated and to be measures of the
same type. More research is needed before a "best" set of definitions can be chosen. At this time, it is strategically more valuable
to explore several sets of definitions.

RELATIONSHIPS AMONG TYPES

The personality types, when assessed by the Vocational Preference Inventory, are moderately intercorrelated with one another.
A knowledge of these intercorrelations serves a number of useful
purposes. First, they are a guide to the consistency of a person's
personality pattern. For example, types 3 and 5 (Social and
Enterprising) are moderately and positively correlated: when
these types constitute the first two peaks in a profile, they indicate
a sociable, dependent character. However, if one is high and
the other low in the profile, we cannot be as certain of the presence of these attributes. Similar interpretations can be made from
other patterns of intercorrelation shown in Table 3. Second, the
size of the intercorrelations are generally consistent with the

formulations for the types. For example, the Intellectual type differs greatly from the Enterprising type in skills, values, orientation toward people; these differences are reflected in the low intercorrelation between measures of these types: r equals $-.04$ and $.03$ for boys and girls respectively.

SUBTYPES AND PERSONALITY PATTERNS

The use of an interest inventory profile enables us to classify people according to their personality pattern, or their resemblance to each of the six personality types. Thus, we can study the various subtypes (that is, people classified by two- to six-digit codes rather than by single digits) to arrive at a more complete understanding of complex personality patterns. For example, persons can be classified as Intellectual-Realistic, Intellectual-Social, Intellectual-Conventional, Intellectual-Enterprising, or Intellectual-Artistic subtypes and then compared for their achievements, goals, resistance to influence, and other behavior. Table

TABLE 3

The Relationships Among the Personality Types As Estimated by Corresponding Scales of the Vocational Preference Inventory

	1 Real	2 Int	3 Soc	4 Conv	5 Ent	6 Art
1 Realistic	—	.49	.06	.21	.14	.17
2 Intellectual	.42	—	.11	.13	.03	.19
3 Social	.26	.22	—	.15	.36	.27
4 Conventional	.35	.20	.25	—	.31	−.09
5 Enterprising	.17	−.04	.44	.54	—	.34
6 Artistic	.19	.29	.46	.07	.35	—

NOTE: Correlations for boys (N = 307) are below the diagonal; those for girls (N = 226) are above the diagonal. Both groups are National Merit Finalists. Similar patterns of relationships can be observed in Strong's data for the SVIB. See Table 29, pp. 136–137 of Vocational Interests of Men and Women [121].

TABLE 4

The Coding of Interest Inventory Scales for the Study of Types and Subtypes

Subject	Type and Scale Names						
	Real	Int	Soc	Conv	Ent	Art	
	Type and Scale Numbers						
	1	2	3	4	5	6	Code
A	10	20	70	60	90	50	53
B	80	90	20	30	40	10	21
C	10	40	50	35	40	85	63

NOTE: The coding of profiles can be elaborated by coding all scales and by including signs to indicate the elevation of various scales. However, these elaborations require extremely large samples for empirical study. For this example, we have coded each subject by the percentile rank of his two highest scores.

4 illustrates the coding of interest inventory scales for the study of single types and subtypes. For example, Subject A, whose highest and next highest scores are Enterprising and Social, respectively, has an Enterprising-Social pattern (which would be coded 53). It seems obvious that the use of subtypes rather than single types will lead to more efficient predictions and greater understanding.

A classification of occupational subtypes and a method for determining subtypes is also presented in Part II of Appendix A. New research is needed to examine the value of these methods.

SUMMARY

The types, which probably represent common outcomes of growing up in our culture, have been described in terms of a theoretical model and an empirical definition. The personality types are models for organizing knowledge, stimulating research, and conceptualizing personality.

CHAPTER THREE

Personality Types
and Expected Performance

Assuming that the conceptual formulations in Chapter Two are valid guesses about the nature of vocational life, what inferences can we draw from them? A review of the formulations suggests a series of hypotheses about several related performances important to both the person and society: (1) vocational choice, job satisfaction, stability, and achievement; (2) academic achievement; (3) creative performance; and (4) personal development and stability. The hypotheses that follow are based on the formulations and are assumed to be consistent with them.

VOCATIONAL CHOICE, JOB SATISFACTION, STABILITY, AND ACHIEVEMENT

A person's vocational choice, stability, and achievement may be conceived of as involving (1) his direction of choice (meaning his choice of a particular field or kind of work) and subsequent changes in that direction, and (2) his level of vocational choice and eventual vocational achievement.

Direction of Choice. A person's *primary* direction of choice may be defined as his choice of one of the six groups of occupations enumerated earlier: Realistic, Intellectual, Social, Conventional,

Enterprising, and Artistic. The primary direction is a function of the dominant characteristic (that is, the model type he most resembles) of his personality pattern.

The *secondary* direction of vocational choice is a function of the secondary characteristic of his personality pattern: that is, the model type that the person resembles secondarily. This secondary direction determines his choice of role within the major vocational class of his choice. For example, a prospective engineer may become a researcher, a supervisor, a teacher, or a consultant in the field of engineering; his preference constitutes the secondary direction. The secondary direction represents a specification —a narrowing or focusing—of choice; it is analogous to "the funnel process" that Hahn and MacLean [59] ascribe to vocational experience. Studies of secondary direction and subsequent development have been made for various vocational groups: engineers [31, 33], psychologists [81, 121], and physicians [49, 122].

Stability and fluctuation in vocational choice are functions of both the dominant characteristics and the consistency of the personality pattern. The choices of Realistic and Intellectual men tend to be stable [67, 68], perhaps because of the nonsociability and insensitivity of the Realistic type and the nonsociability and independence of the Intellectual type. Social, Conventional, Enterprising, and Artistic men are unstable: that is, they tend to change their vocational choices. Possibly the orally dependent and materialistic qualities of the Social, Conventional, and Enterprising types, and the personal instability of the Artistic type foster change. In relation to these findings, it is interesting to note that adolescent boys who report that their daydreams have centered around the same kinds of vocations over a long period of time tend to be Realistic and Intellectual types [69].

These results are corroborated by similar findings obtained in longitudinal studies for the college years. In a study of susceptibility to influence, King [78] finds that his high-persuasibility group, which resembles the Social type, "tends to have a stronger need to maintain close, harmonious social relationships, lower self-esteem, higher overt anxiety, and poorer health."

The consistency of the personality pattern is also positively correlated with stability of vocational choice [68]; that is, some primary-secondary patterns are more conducive to stability than others. People with consistent personality patterns tend to change their direction of choice (move from one vocational class to another) relatively infrequently, whereas people with inconsistent codes have vocational histories characterized by frequent changes.

Consistent codes (obtained from the interest profiles described earlier in Table 4, page 41) include the following combinations: 12, 21, 14, 41, 26, 62, 36, 63, 45, 54, 56, 65, 53, 35, 34, and 43. Inconsistent codes include 23, 32, 24, 42, 16, 61, 25, 52, 46, 64, 13, 31, 15, and 51. The consistency of the code is a function of the similarities between the primary and secondary types. For example, a 21 code (Intellectual-Realistic) is a consistent code, because the model formulations and the empirical evidence indicate that the Intellectual and the Realistic types have many traits in common—unsociability, an orientation toward things rather than people, self-deprecation, and masculinity—although they also have some contradictory attributes. Inconsistent codes are assumed to indicate that the person has psychological attributes that are somewhat contradictory. For example, a 13 (Realistic-Social) code is an inconsistent code, because the models for the Realistic and Social types contain such oppositions as an orientation toward things versus an orientation toward people, masculinity versus femininity, poor interpersonal skills versus good interpersonal skills, motoric skills versus verbal skills. The consistency hypothesis is related in many ways to Festinger's concept of dissonance [38], Lecky's "self-consistency" [86], and Vance and Volsky's "psychological discordance" [134].

Reaction to External Influences. The person whose first choice of vocation is thwarted because of lack of training funds, rejection by his employer, lack of opportunity, or some other external force will select other occupations or positions of the same type if his personality pattern is consistent or if he resembles the Realistic or the Intellectual more than the other four types. For the person with an *inconsistent* pattern, the direction of choice will more frequently be determined by environmental contingencies, because his unstable pattern lessens his self-direction.

In general, resistance to external pressure probably depends somewhat more on the consistency of the personality pattern than on the dominant personality type. A person with a consistent pattern (for instance, a Social-Enterprising type) is less likely to be swayed by external forces than is a person with an inconsistent pattern (for instance, a Social-Intellectual type). Consistent patterns should probably be regarded as integrated patterns—integrated in the sense that they represent similar or complementary values, attitudes, and coping mechanisms. Crites' finding [22] that "ego strength" is positively associated with the presence of interest patterning on the Strong seems to illustrate this phenomenon.

The potency that a particular environmental pressure will exert on a person's direction of choice is a function of the dominant type represented in the personality pattern, the degree to which this type dominates the pattern, and the consistency of the profile. For example, a consistent personality pattern represented by a profile peak on the Intellectual scale followed by a much lower peak on the Realistic scale, and only negligible elevations on the remaining scales, would be both more predictable and more sensitive to those influences which, according to the hypothesis, most strongly affect the Intellectual type. In contrast, a person with an *inconsistent* personality pattern dominated by a profile peak on the Intellectual scale followed by a peak on the Social scale would be less predictable and less sensitive to the influences assumed to affect the Intellectual type. The environmental situations that are likely to be the most and the least influential with each type are as follows.

1. The Realistic type is most susceptible to pragmatic, masculine, and nonsocial influences and least sensitive to social, feminine, and intellectual influences.

2. The Intellectual type is most sensitive to abstract, theoretical, and analytic influences and least sensitive to materialistic and social influences.

3. The Social type is most sensitive to social, humanitarian, and religious influences and least sensitive to abstract or analytic influences.

4. The Conventional type is most sensitive to materialistic and social influences and least sensitive to intellectual and idealistic influences.

5. The Enterprising type is most sensitive to social, emotional, enthusiastic, and materialistic influences and least sensitive to intellectual, humanitarian, and idealistic influences.

6. The Artistic type is most sensitive to personal, emotional and imaginative influences and least sensitive to social, materialistic, and realistic influences.

To determine the effects of one external influence, financial aid, upon vocational choice, students (National Merit Finalists) were asked, "If you had unlimited financial resources, would your first choice be a different one?" Responses were related to the students' dominant personality type in 2 by 6 tables, which were then tested with chi square. Table 5 presents the results for both sexes [67]. As the table shows, 32.7 per cent of the boys with

TABLE 5

Relation Between the Student's High-Point Code and His Response to the Question "If You Had Unlimited Financial Resources, Would Your First Choice Be a Different One?"

Would Change Choice	1 Real	2 Int	3 Soc	4 Conv	5 Ent	6 Art	χ^2
Boys (N = 148)	12.3	7.6	18.5	17.1	32.7	22.0	25.12[*]
Girls (N = 86)	16.4	19.5	9.3	14.8	17.9	32.2	15.94[†]

NOTE: Only 17.8 and 18.7 per cent of the total sample of boys and girls, respectively, indicated they would change their choices if unlimited funds were available. The "high-point code" is the scale on which the person achieves his highest score.

[*] $p < .001$.
[†] $p < .01$.

Enterprising codes said they would change their vocational choice if they had unlimited financial resources, whereas only 7.6 per cent of the students with Intellectual codes said they would change. This extreme contrast seems consistent with the values expressed by persons in each of the two occupational codes. The findings for girls are more ambiguous: girls with Artistic choices would change their goals more readily than girls with Social choices. These differences in susceptibility to external influence may be attributable to cultural biases about the "impracticality" of Artistic occupations and the "practicality" of Social occupations for girls.

Vocational Achievement. In addition to determining the direction of vocational choice, the personality pattern also determines the person's level of vocational aspiration and achievement. A consistent personality pattern makes for effective functioning. We may assume that an integrated pattern makes for stability and integrated effort, and therefore a person with a consistent pattern is more likely to survive at a given kind of work.

People who have not only a consistent pattern but also a close resemblance to the Social or the Enterprising type are likely to have higher aspirations, to achieve more frequently, and to be more occupationally mobile. Other things being equal, people with closer resemblances to these two types achieve more than people with fewer resemblances. (Here "other things" include the person's intelligence and social background, factors that are important determinants of achievement but that are partially incorporated in the types themselves.) No doubt their self-confidence, enthusiasm, and perceptiveness in dealing with others—common requirements for achievement in our culture—account for the greater success of these types.

The level of vocational aspiration is also related to the personality types. Enterprising, Social, and Artistic types tend to overevaluate their potential, and thus to have higher aspirations; Conventional, Intellectual, and Realistic types tend to underrate themselves. We see here a reflection of the "realism hypothesis" frequently discussed in vocational counseling: "unrealistic" vocational aspirations (that is, aspirations that are either too high or too low in terms of a person's ability and potential) are associated with the extremes of overevaluation and underevaluation. Thus, we would expect both the Enterprising and the Realistic types to have "unrealistic" vocational goals.

Moreover, people with consistent codes are more likely to make "realistic" choices and to have reasonable aspirations, because a consistent code implies an integrated person who knows himself well. Consequently, an accurate self-evaluation is one facet of integrity and stability.

Work History (Career Pattern). From the previous statements about stability of vocational choice, we can make certain predictions about the character of the work history. The Realistic and Intellectual types and people with consistent codes will be more vocationally stable (that is, they will change jobs less often) than people who resemble the other four types or people with inconsistent codes.

Work Satisfaction. Expressions of work satisfaction will be associated with consistent rather than inconsistent codes. Persons with inconsistent codes may be expected to express dissatisfaction more often, because they are by definition somewhat dissatisfied and self-contradictory and because they appear to have conflicting motives.

ACADEMIC ACHIEVEMENT

Such other things as intelligence and socioeconomic status being equal, high educational aspirations (as measured by highest academic degree sought) will be positively associated with the model types in the following order: Intellectual, Social, Artistic, Conventional, Enterprising, and Realistic. Educational achievement (as reflected in grades) and satisfaction with educational training will be correlated with the types in about the same order.

The formulations for each type suggest the particular level of educational aspiration, achievement, and satisfaction. For example, the Intellectual type would be expected to have the highest educational aspirations of the six types, because the Intellectual type by definition values intellectual tasks: reading, thinking, writing. In contrast, the Realistic type, who is concerned with action as opposed to thought, would aspire to achievements in the "real" rather than the intellectual world.

The choice of major field, stability in major field, and satisfaction with and achievement in major field will be influenced by personality in the same ways that vocational choice is. (See the previous discussion.)

CREATIVE PERFORMANCE

The field in which a person will perform creatively is determined by the dominant characteristic of his personality pattern. Whatever a person's dominant personality characteristic, the higher the rank of the Artistic and Intellectual types in his profile, the more likely it is that he will perform creatively. This hypothesis rests on the formulations and related evidence that suggest that these types have creative predispositions. For example, a person with a Realistic-Intellectual-Artistic [126] pattern would be expected to perform more originally than a person with a Realistic-Conventional-Artistic-Intellectual [1462] pattern.

Similarly, people with consistent codes are more apt to perform creatively than are people with inconsistent codes, because consistent codes probably foster achievement. Because the Intellectual and the Artistic types are the most creative, and because these two types are consistent with one another, the Intellectual-Artistic and the Artistic-Intellectual patterns probably represent the highest degree of creative performance. At the other extreme, a Realistic-Enterprising pattern would be especially uncreative, because this pattern is inconsistent and because the individual types lack creative potential.

Other things—such as field or vocation, consistency of codes, and environmental pressures—being equal, the specific nature of the created product will be predictable from the personality pattern. For example, people with patterns of 261 (Intellectual-Artistic-Realistic) would be expected to develop ingenious mechanical apparatus, whereas people with patterns of 263 (Intellectual-Artistic-Social) would be expected to develop ingenious social techniques, imaginative social theories, and similar socially oriented products. This kind of analysis is analogous to Weissman's method of profile analysis of the Strong [138], which he used to study the "intellectual disposition" of students by arranging students along an applied-theoretical interest continuum.

PERSONAL DEVELOPMENT AND STABILITY

Because the various types differ in their developmental histories and adult personalities, they probably differ in their proneness to behavior disorders. We may hypothesize that the Realistic type (who is literally that: reality-oriented) is the least apt to develop adjustment problems, whereas the Artistic type (because of the very qualities that make him "artistic") is the most likely. There is some evidence to support this hypothesis [41, 47, 101], although much of the evidence is contradictory.

The differences among types with respect to history, adult personality, and perceptual outlook imply also that they respond differentially to various kinds of psychiatric treatment. For example, the Realistic and Conventional types might be expected to respond well to treatments that involve explicit authoritative manipulation of the soma through drugs, physical therapies, and activity. The Social type, and to a lesser degree the Enterprising type, because of their orientation toward people and their verbal skills, would probably respond well to individual and group psychotherapy. The Artistic type, although by definition more unstable than the others, would also be amenable to individual psychotherapy because of his habit of using his primitive and childish impulses. The Intellectual type would be only a fair prospect for individual psychotherapy because of his ability to erect intricate barriers that neither he nor his therapist can easily break through.

SUMMARY

This chapter spells out some of the obvious implications of the formulations for the personality types. The models can be used for constructing hypotheses about a number of other human problems. For example, we might ask what kind of leadership is ideal for each model? If we wanted to bring about changes in certain institutions and practices—childrearing, teaching, business organizations—what appeals will be most effective in reaching each of the types? Why have labor unions been relatively successful among Realistic persons, but unsuccessful among Social and Conventional persons? Provisional answers to these and other questions can be inferred from the model formulations.

CHAPTER FOUR

The Environmental Models

HUMAN BEHAVIOR depends upon *both* personality *and* the specific environment in which a person lives. The model formulations yield helpful information about people, but that information is incomplete unless we find some way to characterize the environment as well as the person. Murray's early study [96] of personal "needs" and environmental "presses" is a useful illustration of this idea. Therefore, to supplement the model personality types, we have proposed six model environments to characterize the common physical and social environments in our culture. The model environments correspond to the personality types: thus, for each personality type there is a related environment.

Just as we can assess real people by comparing them with the personality types, so we can assess real environments by comparing them with model environments—that is, descriptions of hypothetical environments. Both the environmental models and the personality types are derived from the same concepts. The six personality types—Realistic, Intellectual, Social, Conventional, Enterprising, and Artistic—reflect vocational preferences; the formulations in Chapter Two explain the meaning of these preferences and their relations to personal traits. In turn, environmental models may be defined as the situation or atmosphere created by the people who dominate a given environment. For instance, a Realistic environment would be an environment dominated by Realistic types.

Because the personality types and the environmental models share a common set of constructs, it is possible to classify people and environments in the same terms and thus to predict the outcome of pairing people and environments. More explicitly: to predict what will happen when a particular person is put into a particular environment, we need only to characterize the person and his environment in terms of the models and to review the appropriate formulations in order to discover the congruities and incongruities the models suggest. For example, the interaction of a Realistic type and a Realistic environment should produce a number of desirable outcomes, such as work satisfaction, achievement, and vocational stability.* Our typology gives us a tremendous advantage both in planning research and in interpreting results. Without it, we would have to deal with a formidable number of possible person–environment interactions; with it, we have relatively few variables to juggle and an explicit rationale to guide us.

The construction of the model environments rests mainly on the suggestion made by Linton [89] and others that most of our environment is transmitted through other people. This idea implies that the character of an environment is dependent upon the nature of its members, and that the *dominant* features of an environment are dependent upon the *typical* characteristics of its members. If we know what kind of people make up a group, then, we can infer the climate that the group creates. For example, an office full of engineers would be expected to have a different atmosphere than an office full of accountants. Or, an informal gathering of salesmen would differ in atmosphere from an informal gathering of ministers.

A large portion of the model environment consists of those attributes of the model types that affect others. In addition, because model types are characterized by a preference for special tasks and situations, the description of model environments by means of model types results in the delineation of tasks and

* Chapters Five and Six provide a complete account of the explanatory values of the theory for these purposes.

situations thought to be associated with and congenial to the different personality types.

The descriptions of the model environments in this chapter follow the plan for the model types: Conceptual definition; empirical definition; empirical characterization in terms of typical tasks, situations, and interpersonal relationships; and conceptual formulation. The information about occupational environments was obtained from Fine's United States Employment Service study of 4000 jobs [39, 132]. This information was sorted into six categories, using the lists of occupations shown in Table 1. A tally of the attributes characteristic of each of the six occupational classes was then made. In this way, it was possible to secure the typical characteristics for each occupational class or model environment. In addition, hypotheses about other probable attributes and their effects were made after a careful review of Fine's data. Because Fine's classification and the present selection of information are in the last analysis subjective (Fine used experienced employment men), the reader should realize that the environmental models are just that—speculative formulations rather than empirical summaries.

The Realistic Environment

Conceptual Definition. The Realistic environment is characterized by the explicit, physical, concrete tasks with which it confronts its inhabitants. Effective solutions often require mechanical ingenuity and skill, persistence, and physical movement from place to place, often outdoors. The Realistic environment demands only minimal interpersonal skills, because most of the tasks it sets can be accomplished by superficial and casual relationships that frequently require only stereotyped conversations. Tasks frequently call for simple sets of action. The explicit quality of the environmental demands make "success" and "failure" almost immediately obvious.

Empirical Definition. The Realistic environment is populated largely by persons who have preferences for, are training for, or are employed in such occupations as airplane mechanic, construction inspector, electrician, filling station attendant, and fish and wildlife specialist.* The following settings are typical of the Realistic environment: a filling station, a machine shop, a farm, a construction project, a barber shop.

Empirical Characterization. Typical Problems and Situations: Typically the problems are mechanical, demanding the use of tools and machines. Solutions frequently must be reached within established limits of time and physical tolerance. Such tasks demand carefulness, close attention, speed, and persistence. Work activities are typically nonsocial and are carried on in relation to processes, machines, and techniques, both indoors and outdoors. Work activities are occasionally physically hazardous. Work tasks often require medium to great capacity for such physical activities as reaching, handling, fingering, feeling, and seeing.

Interpersonal Relationships: Minimal social skills are demanded, and these are usually limited to receiving or giving explicit information and playing a masculine role. Need for sensitivity or perceptiveness toward others is minimal. The persons in this environment are "realistic"; thus, a person introduced into the Realistic environment is surrounded by people whose values, aptitudes, and personalities are conventional, materialistic, and masculine. A person new to the Realistic environment, then, needs some ability to cope with the Realistic person. Presumably, similarity between the inhabitants and the newcomer will make for effective interpersonal relations.

The Intellectual Environment

Conceptual Definition. The Intellectual environment is characterized by tasks that require abstract and creative abilities rather than personal perceptiveness. Effective solutions require imagination, intelligence, and sensitivity to physical and intellectual problems. Achievement is usually gradual, taking place over a prolonged period of time, although the criteria of achievement may be objective and measurable. The problems posed by

* See Chapter Two for a complete list of these criteria and of the criteria for the other five classes.

the environment vary in their level of difficulty: solutions to simple problems can sometimes be obtained by the direct application of past training, whereas solutions to more complex problems require persistence and originality. Tools and apparatus require intellectual more than manual skills. Writing ability is frequently necessary.

Empirical Definition. The Intellectual environment is populated mostly by persons who have preferences for, are training for, or are employed in such occupations as aeronautical design engineer, anthropologist, astronomer, biologist, and botanist. The following settings are typical of the Intellectual environment: a research laboratory; a diagnostic case conference in a hospital or clinic; a library; work groups of scientists, research engineers, or mathematicians; studies and offices with books or scientific apparatus.

Empirical Characterization. Typical Problems and Situations: Work is with ideas and things rather than with other people. Relationships with others are superficial rather than close. Scientific problems usually have standards, tolerances, and limits, but these limits are less explicit than those necessary for achievement in the Realistic or Conventional environments. Laboratory equipment is used in the service of intellectual or scientific problems rather than in the performance of mechanical solutions, as is the case in the Realistic environment. The physical requirements are light: talking, reading, and verbal and ideational learning. Work activities usually take place indoors.

Interpersonal Relationships: Minimal social skills are demanded, although ability to give and receive complicated written and oral instructions is necessary. Need for sensitivity to the needs and problems of others is minimal. Ability to relate effectively to Intellectual types is helpful in achieving personal goals and acquiring vocational status, because the Intellectual environment is populated principally by Intellectual types.

The Social Environment

Conceptual Definition. The Social environment is characterized by problems that require the ability to interpret and modify human behavior and an interest in caring for and communicating with others. Generally, the work situations foster self-esteem and convey status.

Empirical Definition. The Social environment is populated largely by persons who have preferences for, are training for, or are employed in such occupations as assistant city school superintendent, clinical psychologist, director of welfare agency, foreign missionary, and high school teacher. The following settings are typical of the Social environment: school and college classrooms, counseling or therapeutic interviewing offices, mental hospitals, churches, educational offices, and recreation centers.

Empirical Characterization. Typical Problems and Situations: The ability to interpret human behavior and to teach others is required. Principal work situations require frequent, prolonged personal relationships with others. Those persons receiving help or training convey status and affection to the person working in this environment. Work hazards are emotional because relatively close relationships with students, employees, and patients may stir up those conflicts and feelings that have been poorly resolved. Verbal facility is demanded for lecturing, teaching, and helping others. Physical requirements are light: talking, reading, and listening.

Interpersonal Relationships: High degree of social sensitivity and skill is demanded. Ability to interpret and cope with a great range of types, including other Social types, is required.

The Conventional Environment

Conceptual Definition. The Conventional environment is characterized by tasks and problems that require systematic, concrete, routine processing of verbal and mathematical information. Successful solutions are relatively explicit and occur in relatively short periods of time. More complex problems in this environment require managing the activities of others or directing an entire operation.

Empirical Definition. The Conventional environment is populated largely by persons who have preferences for, are training for, or are employed in such occupations as bank examiner, bank teller, bookkeeper, budget reviewer, and cost estimator. The following settings are typical of the Conventional environment: a bank, an accounting firm, a post office, a file room, and a business office.

Empirical Characterization. Typical Problems and Situations: Tasks frequently call for repetitive, short-cycle operations carried out according to set procedures or sequences. Activities are routine, concrete, organized. Regular duties require reaching, handling, fingering, feeling, and seeing. Little physical strength is required.

Interpersonal Relationships: Regular duties require minimal interpersonal skills, because the majority of time is spent working with things and materials. Interpersonal relationships can be coped with in a relatively superficial manner and without much personal involvement or feeling. The Conventional environment requires the ability to cope with Conventional types, who are characterized by their economic values, self-control, and passivity.

The Enterprising Environment

Conceptual Definition. The Enterprising environment is characterized by tasks that place a premium on verbal facility used to direct or persuade other people.

Empirical Definition. The Enterprising environment is populated largely by persons who have preferences for, are training for, or are employed in such occupations as business executive, buyer, hotel manager, industrial relations consultant, and manufacturer's representative. The following settings are typical of the Enterprising environment: a car lot, a real-estate office, a political rally, and an advertising agency.

Empirical Characterization. Typical Problems and Situations: Tasks typically require directing, controlling, and planning the activities of others. Persuasive and supervisory roles usually draw esteem and respect from other people. The environment requires an interest in people and things. Because most work activities are people-oriented, social skills are needed. The most important physical requirements relate to talking and listening.

Interpersonal Relationships: The ability to relate to a great variety of other people in many different situations is frequently necessary. Likewise, the ability to perceive the motives of others in order to lead and persuade is essential. Unlike the Social environment, this environment does not call for the ability to form close relationships that tax emotional resources. Finally, this environment requires the ability to cope with Enterprising types, who are competitive, aggressive, and materialistic.

The Artistic Environment

Conceptual Definition. The Artistic environment is characterized by tasks and problems that require the interpretation or creation of artistic forms through taste, feelings, and imagination. The most complex tasks require great tolerance for ambiguity and imagination. The simpler tasks require chiefly a sense of excellence or fitness. The Artistic environment requires the ability to draw upon all of one's knowledge, intuition, and emotional life in problem solving; in contrast, the Realistic, Intellectual, and Conventional environments frequently demand less use of a person's total resources.

Empirical Definition. The Artistic environment is populated mostly by persons who have preferences for, are training for, or are employed in such occupations as art dealer, author, cartoonist, commercial artist, and composer. The following settings are typical of the Artistic environment: a play rehearsal, a concert hall, a dance studio, a study, a library, a garret.

Empirical Characterization. Typical Problems and Situations: Tasks typically require the interpretation of feelings, ideas, or facts in terms of a personal viewpoint. Information is evaluated against sensory or judgmental criteria. Standards of excellence are demanded, but their definitions are often ambiguous. The Artistic environment demands intense involvement over long periods of time. Some Artistic activities (drama) involve close working relationships, whereas others (painting) are carried out in almost complete isolation.

ASSESSMENT CRITERIA

Because many of the psychologically important features of the environment consist of or are transmitted by the people in it, we can, in principle, characterize an environment by assessing its population. The Environmental Assessment Technique (EAT) was developed for this purpose. This technique entails a census of the occupations, training preferences, or vocational preferences of a population; the population may be that of a college, a hospital, a business, a community, or any other group. These preferences or occupations are classified on the basis of the criteria for the classes as belonging to one of the six environments. This classification results in a six-variable profile. The absolute numbers for each type are then converted to percentages of the total population for the particular environment or institution. For example, a business consisting of 100 employees might have the following distribution of types:

Type No.	Type	Number	Per Cent
1	Realistic	10	10
2	Intellectual	4	4
3	Social	6	6
4	Conventional	64	64
5	Enterprising	14	14
6	Artistic	2	2

Its environmental pattern would be represented by the code 451326, because the dominant type in this environment is the Conventional (type 4), followed by the Enterprising (type 5). Such an environment would be expected to emphasize orderliness, social status, conservative economic and political beliefs, and similar presses.

Similar codes can be obtained for colleges by a census and categorization of the proportion of students in different major fields. Studies by Astin and Holland [9] and by Astin [8] indicate that such a technique has moderate validity and high retest reliability over a one-year interval. For the six Environmental Assessment Technique variables, retest coefficients range from .81 to .99. To test the validity of this method, profiles of 335 colleges were obtained; these profiles were based on the percentage of students majoring in fields in each of the six areas. Then the percentages were correlated with reports by other groups of students who rated their colleges on the College Characteristics Index [99].

In general, the results were positive. For example, colleges with large percentages of Realistic students (engineering and agricultural majors) tended to be rated low on Humanism, high on Pragmatism, low on Sentience (capacity for feeling experience), and low on Reflectiveness. Colleges with large percentages of Social students (education majors) were described on the College Characteristics Inventory as having a narcissistic, sexual, exhibitionistic, and *anti*scientific atmosphere.

In a second study, similar results were obtained [8]. In short, these studies suggest that a census of the kinds of people found at a college provides a useful index of the atmosphere or climate of the college.

More recently in a factor analysis of institutional variables at 335 colleges, Astin [5] found five factors that were similar to five of the six Environmental Assessment Technique variables. His study suggests that the simple census of a college provided by the Environmental Assessment Technique is related to a great variety of institutional characteristics: faculty attributes, financial status, size, control, and similar objective attributes.

Astin has also refined the Environmental Assessment Technique [8] by weighting each vocation or major for the *two* types it resembles. This refinement may lead to more discriminating assessments than those provided by assigning a vocation to a single type.

Presumably, we can assess environments other than colleges. For instance, communities could be assessed using information from the government census. Such assessments might make possible cross-cultural comparisons. Close human relationships, such as the one between parents and child, could be studied by categorizing the significant person as a kind of one-man environment.

SUMMARY

The model environments are useful in suggesting research and in categorizing the character of an environment. It is assumed that environments can be characterized by a six-variable typology that will provide a simple, empirical tool especially helpful for predicting and understanding the various outcomes of a given person's being placed in a given environment.

CHAPTER FIVE

Environmental Models and Expected Influences

LIKE THE MODEL personality types, the model environments imply many hypotheses about a person's vocational, academic, creative, and personal performance. The following hypotheses are derived from the model formulations (Chapter Four regarded simply as axiomatic statements from which certain inferences can be drawn.

To facilitate comparisons, the following sections on the implications of the environmental models follow the same sequence as the discussion of the implications of the personality types (Chapter Three).

VOCATIONAL BEHAVIOR

The implications of the model environments for the direction of vocational choice, stability of choice, vocational achievement, work history (career pattern), and job satisfaction are as follows:

Direction of Vocational Choice. Each model environment attracts or is sought out by that person whose dominant type is similar to the type associated with the environment. Realistic environments attract Realistic types; Intellectual environments attract Intellectual types. This hypothesis, which is based on the notion that friendships grow out of similar interests and values, should be qualified: The person is attracted also to those tasks and situations that gratify his personal needs and give him satisfaction.

There is some tentative support for the hypothesis that attraction to a group is a function of the satisfaction of needs provided by membership in the group [120]. The converse also seems true. Libo [88] found that people regard as unattractive those groups in which they have to discuss topics uninteresting to them.

Individual items from various interest inventories illustrate the attraction of environmental presses. In the Strong Vocational Interest Blank, for example, the subject is given an opportunity to express his preference for various kinds of supervision, for opportunity to use his knowledge and experience, for opportunity for promotion, for opportunity to seek help about difficulties, and for similar environmental attributes.

Table 6 shows the degree of positive and negative attractiveness that the different environments have to each personal type. This table makes explicit the hypothesis that a given environment

TABLE 6

The Attractiveness of the Model Environments to Different Personality Types

Personality Types	Model Environments					
	1 Real	2 Int	3 Soc	4 Conv	5 Ent	6 Art
1 Realistic	++	+	−	−	−	−−
2 Intellectual	+	++	−	−	−−	+
3 Social	−−	−	++	−	+	+
4 Conventional	−	−	+	++	+	−−
5 Enterprising	−	−−	+	−	++	+
6 Artistic	−	−	+	−−	−	++

NOTE: (++) equals "very attractive." (+) equals "attractive." (−) equals "unattractive." (−−) equals "very unattractive." This table should also be interpreted as showing the degree of congruency for various person–environment interactions.

TABLE 7

The Role Demands of Different Environments

Roles	Environmental Models					
	1 Real	2 Int	3 Soc	4 Conv	5 Ent	6 Art
Practitioner	1	2	1	1	4	1
Teacher or therapist	5	4	2	4	3	4
Leader or supervisor	2	5	3	2	1	5
Expert or consultant	3	3	6	3	5	3
Researcher	4	1	5	5	6	2
Multiple roles	6	6	4	6	2	6

NOTE: 1 indicates role most in demand; 6 indicates role least in demand.

will have a somewhat different potency for each personality type as a function of the degree of similarity between the personality type and the environmental model. A Social type in a Social environment will find he is surrounded by other Social types who, like himself, enjoy talking and teaching others. Moreover, he finds that he is in an environment where he can avoid mechanical and mathematical problems—tasks he finds distasteful.

Environments press their members to assume particular roles: a given environment exerts upon the person different degrees of pressure for different roles. Table 7 shows the ordering of role demands within the various environments. To elaborate, the environments not only present special tasks and situations but also attract or repel persons by emphasizing special roles. A Realistic environment, for instance, most frequently demands that a person play the role of a practitioner of his trade. Only infrequently does it demand that a person play the role of a teacher or a therapist. Accordingly, a person who likes the role of the skilled tradesman and who dislikes or feels threatened by the role of teacher will find the Realistic environment congenial. To take another example, a person who likes to be a teacher or a leader, or to adopt multiple roles rather than limiting himself to one, and who dis-

likes studious or intellectual roles—expert, consultant, researcher
—will find the Enterprising environment a satisfying one, because
in it he can play the roles he favors and escape those he dislikes.

Stability of Choice. An environment affects stability of vocational choice by virtue of both its special character and its consistency. The Realistic environments are probably conducive to
stability because they offer many explicit or immediate satisfactions. A carpenter, for example, can see the immediate results of
his craftsmanship; he can make rapid checks to learn if his work
conforms to standards (blueprints); and he can show his work
to others.

In contrast, the Social, Enterprising, and Artistic environments
are not conducive to stability of vocational choice and goals for
at least two reasons: First, explicit signs of achievement are un-
common. Second, the complexity of the problems involved—the
manipulation of other people or of artistic media—make "successful performance" difficult to attain. The sophisticated teacher,
for instance, can rarely be sure which techniques will prove
effective in teaching students; nor, in the case of failure, can he
know whether the fault lies in him, in the students, or in some
extraneous factor that interfered with teaching effectiveness. The
work of the psychotherapist is even more elusive. He is not sure
of what he starts with—the patient's true condition—and he is
not sure what creates growth, what blocks therapeutic progress,
or even whether to believe the patient's reports of progress or
failure.

Both the consistency and the homogeneity of an environment
are positively correlated with stability of vocational choice. A
"consistent" environment is one whose environmental pattern is
psychologically and sociologically consistent. The "environmental
pattern" is the profile of types obtained from the census of all
types in an environment. The two-digit codes considered consistent personality patterns also indicate consistent environmental
patterns. (See page 44.)

A consistent environment is assumed to foster stability because
it exerts pressure for unified or complementary goals, roles, and
coping behavior. The divergent attributes of the inconsistent en-

vironment press for diverse goals, roles, and coping behavior; in short, the pressures conflict. This conflict activates the doubts and conflicts of the person in the environment. Thus, a consistent environment helps the person who is ambivalent about his choice to suppress his uncertainties, whereas an inconsistent environment not only prevents the person from suppressing his doubts but even encourages him to reconsider other plans by providing concrete alternatives that sometimes represent the poles of his conflict. For example, a boy who is majoring in physics but is uncertain about his choice, having considered art as as an alternative, will be moved to reconsider his decision if he is attending a college with a strong art department.

Homogeneous environments are also conducive to vocational stability. A "homogeneous" environment is one that has only one or two dominant environmental presses and four or five very weak environmental presses. Empirically, homogeneity is estimated as the difference in percentage between the highest and lowest types in the environmental profile. Homogeneity is positively correlated with consistency but is not identical with it: consistency refers to the structure of the environment, whereas homogeneity is in essence an intensity measure. It seems likely that a homogeneous environment encourages stability because it exposes its members to one single, strong, integrated press. Other environmental presses, being insignificant, have little influence. For example, technological institutions are usually homogeneous, because engineering departments clearly dominate such institutions. The small islands of the humanities, if they exist at all at such institutions, exert little influence.

Vocational Achievement. The environmental pattern and its individual components considered separately have differential influences on a person's vocational achievement. Each of the six environmental types, considered separately, encourages the kind of vocational achievement associated with that kind of environment. The Social environment fosters social achievements; the Artistic environment fosters artistic achievements.

A consistent and homogeneous environmental profile is probably conducive to vocational achievement. Consistency is assumed to limit the number of different *kinds* of achievements that an environment presses for; homogeneity is assumed to increase the *intensity* of the environmental press for a particular kind of achievement. For example, a student at a technological institute finds himself in a consistent environment that presses principally for scientific and technological goals rather than for a broad range of goals, as a large state university does. The homogeneity of this environment makes the pressure more intense; nearly everybody is striving for the same goals. To strive for other goals or to express doubts about the value of scientific and technological goals is to swim against the current of student and faculty opinion.

Work History (Career Patterns). The nature of the environmental influences upon a person's work history can be inferred from the earlier statements concerning stability of vocational choice. Over a period of time, the number of jobs held by a person in a homogeneous and consistent environment, or in the Realistic or Intellectual environment, will be relatively few. In contrast, a person in a heterogeneous or an inconsistent environment, or in Social, Conventional, Enterprising, or Artistic environments, will change jobs relatively often.

Work Satisfaction. Expressions of vocational satisfaction will be associated more frequently with consistent than with inconsistent codes and with some environmental models more than others. The person in a consistent environment may feel satisfaction simply because, being in an environment that is free from contradictory presses, he knows what to expect. The Social and Enterprising environments may provide satisfaction because they convey prestige on their members—that is, occupations in these environments generally carry more status than occupations in other environments. This hypothesis is modified by another, that satisfaction is positively related to the explicitness of achievement or successful accomplishment. Because the signs of success in such occupations as teaching or therapy are intangible, the person in a Social environment may feel less satisfaction than does a file clerk or a typist in the Conventional environment, where achievement is tangible and definite. It is hard to know which factor—status conferred or lack of explicitness of achievement—has more weight for the person in a Social or an Enterprising environment.

So far, we have talked as if an environment exerted a uniform influence on all its members. Yet obviously the effect of a particular environment will depend upon the person involved. To revert to the previous example: the status conveyed by the Social and the Enterprising environments will have little or no effect upon people who are not concerned with status. Presumably, there are a number of such personal differences that neither the personality types nor the environmental models can cope with adequately. Hopefully, new research and new ideas will lead to more certain knowledge.

ACADEMIC ACHIEVEMENT

The various environments influence academic achievement in different ways, depending on the aspirations and attributes of the types populating each environment. Environments can be ranked from those thought to be most conducive to academic achievement to those that seem least conducive: Intellectual, Social, Conventional, Artistic, Realistic, Enterprising. The Intellectual environment, by definition, encourages academic achievement most. The common concerns of that environment—thinking, reading, writing, and their associated values—press for scholarly work and achievement. The Enterprising environment is least conducive to academic achievement, because it places a premium on activity, aggressiveness, sociability, and their associated values. Such influences interfere with academic achievement.

CREATIVE PERFORMANCE

The various environments foster creativity in different media and to different degrees. The climate for and ethos about creative work vary considerably from environment to environment. Environments are thought to foster creative performance in the following descending order: Artistic, Intellectual, Social, Enterprising, Realistic, and Conventional. The Artistic environment generally demands that the person work without much direction or structure. To survive, he must be able to create esthetically pleasing forms in one or more media of self-expression. Members and prospective members of the Artistic environment are well aware that it demands creative performance. Therefore, these demands serve to attract people with creative potential and to stimulate such people to create after they become members of the environment. In contrast, the Conventional environment discourages creative performance by its excessive structure, its suppression of self-expression, and its recruitment of people who prefer structure to freedom.

PERSONAL DEVELOPMENT AND STABILITY

Because the model environments provide different kinds of gratifications, tasks, and interpersonal relationships, it is likely that they foster personal development and stability in different ways and to different degrees. The Realistic and Conventional environments are thought to be conducive to personal stability because of the concrete, explicit satisfactions and tasks they provide, even though they frequently deny personal expression. The Artistic environment, because of its general character and because of the ambiguity of its criteria of achievement, is probably more conducive to personal instability than any of the other environments. The Intellectual, Social, and Enterprising environments fall between these extremes.

SUMMARY

This attempt to spell out the implications of the model environments is grossly incomplete. No doubt a variety of other hypotheses about the nature of environments will be apparent to readers interested in different outcomes of person–environment interactions. Only further research will show whether or not the environmental models will prove useful in studying parent–child relationships, communities, labor unions, business and professional organizations, and other environments.

CHAPTER SIX

People in Environments

THIS CHAPTER DESCRIBES what happens when a particular kind of person is put into a particular environment. The principal assumptions underlying these hypotheses are, first, that more precise predictions about human behavior can be made by assessing both the person and the environment; and, second, that if the models for the personal types and environments are valid, these models can be used to derive a set of useful hypotheses about the outcomes of pairing persons and environments.

The hypotheses about person–environment interactions are of two main kinds: those having to do with *congruent* interactions, which involve the pairing of a person and his corresponding environment (a Realistic type in a Realistic environment, an Intellectual type in an Intellectual environment, and so on); and those having to do with *incongruent* interactions, which involve the pairing of a person and a more or less dissimilar environment (a Realistic type in an Intellectual environment, a Social type in an Intellectual environment, and so on). It is obvious that congruent interactions strongly reinforce a person's behavior, because he lives with others like himself and engages in tasks tailor-made to suit his aptitudes, values, and favorite methods for dealing with problems. The effects of incongruent interactions are more complicated; however, certain hypotheses about the possible outcomes of such pairings can be inferred. Thus, the theory provides a way to study crude differences in person–

environment "strain" and to formulate hypotheses about the nature of such strains and their relation to anxiety and changes in behavior.

Earlier work by Stern, Stein, and Bloom [115] and Sanford [109] dealt with this question of the psychological "fit" of person and environment. They proposed that some minimal stress is probably necessary for stimulating people to change and to cope with environmental problems. If the environment and person are an exact fit, then the need for change is negligible. But if the person and environment are slightly incompatible, the resultant stress stirs the person to act constructively. However, if the person and the environment are so grossly incompatible that the person cannot, even with great effort, succeed, then such an interaction becomes destructive.

CONGRUENT–INCONGRUENT INTERACTIONS

Generally, congruent person–environment interactions (that is, interactions of people and environments belonging to the same type or model), in contrast to incongruent interactions, are conducive to the following personal performance: (1) more stable vocational choice, (2) higher vocational achievement, (3) higher academic achievement, (4) better maintenance of personal stability, and (5) greater satisfaction. Presumably, congruent interactions produce these outcomes because by definition they involve situations where the tasks and problems presented by the environment are well suited to the person's coping abilities. For example, a salesman (Enterprising type) in an Enterprising environment finds that his interpersonal skills and his need for social interaction are given frequent opportunity for expression and satisfaction. Equally important, the Enterprising environment minimizes the tasks he dislikes—academic, mechanical, and clerical problems. Moreover, he can play the roles he prefers—the leader, the persuader—and avoid the roles he dislikes—the follower, the researcher, the intellectual.

There is an extensive literature to support the hypothesis that a person is more likely to remain in his field of study or his occupation and to achieve vocationally when his interests (personality pattern) are congruent with his environment [10, 18, 19, 36, 51, 75, 77, 90, 92, 108, 115, 119, 121, 136]. In recent studies, Astin [7] and Holland [67, 68] have shown that a student is less likely to change his major field in college if that field is congruent with the dominant feature of his college environment. Astin's study of Ph.D. aspiration [6] also suggests that to some extent the congruency of student and college is conducive to high educational aspiration. The results of these studies are encouraging in that they suggest that the Environmental Assessment Technique variables (which correspond to the six model environments) are measures of some of the most potent forces in the college environment. Further, many of Astin's findings are consistent with our theoretical expectations.

The effects of various person–environment incongruencies were outlined earlier in Table 6. The predictions of performance shown in Table 6 were obtained by comparing the formulations for the personal types with those for the model environments. Because some of the personal types (and, of course, the model environments too) are closely related to one another, the degree of incongruency varies: that is, a particular personal type will find some environments more incompatible than others. For example, a Realistic type is less out of place in a Conventional environment than he is in an Enterprising environment. In addition, each specific interaction produces a different set of outcomes: that is, a particular personal type, confronted by different tasks, settings, and persons to cope with in each of the incongruent environments, will perform differently in each. For example, a mechanic (Realistic type) would feel uncomfortable and incompetent in both a business office (Conventional environment) and an art studio (Artistic environment), but he would feel more uncomfortable in the art studio.

CONSISTENT–INCONSISTENT INTERACTIONS

Because consistent codes imply psychological integration, it is assumed that the pairing of consistent persons and consistent environments is conducive to stability of vocational choice, vocational achievement, academic achievement, personal stability, and satisfaction with vocational choice.

We can further assume that when a person with a consistent personality type (for instance, a 12 code) is placed in an environment which is consistent and congruent (a 12 environment), his performance will be high. Similarly, the interaction of an inconsistent personal type (code 13) and an inconsistent environment (code 24) will lead to such outcomes as dissatisfaction with and changes in vocational choice, lack of academic and vocational achievement, and personal instability. When types and environments are treated as two- to six-digit profiles, the number of possible interactions is extremely large. In the case of two-digit codes, there are 30 possible permutations for the personality pattern and 30 possible permutations for the environmental pattern. Thus, for the two-digit codes alone, 900 combinations of person–environment interactions are possible! Predictions for all possible combinations and permutations of personal and environmental codes can be arrived at by reviewing and comparing consistent and inconsistent codes defined and listed earlier (pages 43–44).

Using six scales of the Strong to represent the types, Holland [68] found that the consistency of a student's code was related to his remaining in a major field over a four-year period. Consistency was also related to achievement, but these findings were equivocal. In addition, students with consistent codes who attended colleges with consistent codes (as measured by the EAT) were more stable in their major field than were any other student–college combination.

HOMOGENEOUS–HETEROGENEOUS INTERACTIONS

The chief effect of pairing a homogeneous type and a homogeneous environment is to make the expected outcomes even more probable. To be more specific: we have hypothesized that the interaction of a consistent type and a consistent environment is conducive to vocational achievement (as well as to other desirable outcomes); if either the personality type or the environment is homogeneous as well as consistent, then vocational achievement is even more likely. *Homogeneity* means the magnitude of the difference between the highest and lowest scores on the six variables used to determine a person's or an environment's degree of resemblance to a personality type or an environmental model. The greater the difference between the highest and lowest of the six scores, the greater the homogeneity. Graphically, the profile of a homogeneous pattern will have high peaks and low valleys; the profile of a heterogeneous pattern will appear rel-

FIGURE 1

Identical Personality Patterns with Different Degrees of Homogeneity

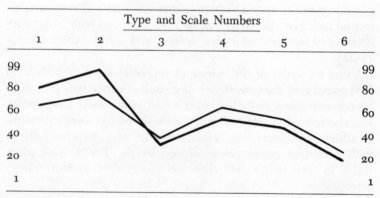

NOTE: Code for A = 214536   Homogeneity = 79
      Code for B = 214536   Homogeneity = 40

atively flat. Figure 1 shows two identical and consistent personality patterns that have different degrees of homogeneity.

In Figure 1, person A, who has a more homogeneous personality pattern than person B, would be more likely to exhibit the performances and attributes associated with the Intellectual-Realistic pattern. Similarly, when a person with a highly homogeneous Intellectual-Realistic pattern interacts with an environment that has the same pattern and is also homogeneous, the effects are more predictable and more intense than are the effects of an interaction between a person and an environment of the same pattern but of less homogeneity.

COMBINATIONS OF CONGRUENCY, CONSISTENCY, AND HOMOGENEITY

It is assumed that interactions involving different degrees of congruency, consistency, and homogeneity will result in different kinds and degrees of outcomes. At one extreme, the interaction of a type and a model environment that are congruent, consistent, and homogeneous will intensify and make more predictable such outcomes as vocational choice and stability, vocational and academic achievement, personal stability, and perhaps creative performance. For example, a Social-Artistic person whose pattern is consistent and homogeneous, and who enters a Social-Artistic environment that has a high degree of homogeneity, will probably be an effective, satisfied person. At the other extreme, incongruency, inconsistency, and heterogeneity make for uncertain predictions and undesirable outcomes: instability in vocational choice, low academic and vocational achievement, personal instability, and lack of creative performance. For example, an Intellectual-Conventional person (an inconsistent pattern) with a low degree of homogeneity who enters a Social-Realistic environment (an inconsistent environment) with a low degree of homogeneity would be expected to be ineffective and dissatisfied.

We do not know if the influences of these characteristics—congruency, consistency, and homogeneity—are equal or differential, because we have not definitely established their validity as individual phenomena or estimated empirically their relative predictive power. To determine their relative influence, further research is required. Up to now, studies have sought to learn only whether or not these characteristics taken individually have statistically significant effects.

SUMMARY

The outcomes associated with the interactions of congruent, consistent, and homogeneous persons and environments have been outlined. Generally, it is assumed that congruent, consistent, and homogeneous interactions have more potent and predictable effects than do incongruent, inconsistent, and heterogeneous interactions. Some evidence in the psychological literature supports the validity of these assertions.

CHAPTER SEVEN

Life Histories

PREVIOUS CHAPTERS were concerned primarily with viewing persons and environments at a single point in time. In this chapter, we will examine changes in human behavior over extended periods of time: the life history. For our purpose, *life history* (or *work history*, as we shall sometimes call it)* may be regarded as representing a particular pattern of living: what Adler has termed *life style*.

By using the definitions of the personality types and model environments, we can, theoretically, trace a person's development from the time he can express a vocational preference to his death and examine the principal environments in which he lives during his entire lifetime. The person can be assessed by his vocational preferences at different points in his life. His environments—family background, school, work situations, and so on—can be assessed using the environmental models. Although this theoretical orientation has been little used, it has promise. By applying the theory, with its small number of classes and relatively simple sets of definitions, to an entire life span, we can utilize a great range of information about human behavior and

---

* The terms *life history* and *work history* seem preferable to *career* or *career pattern*. The concept of career is not sufficiently comprehensive. Wilensky [139], for example, writes, "When the idea of career is taken seriously and applied to large populations, we see that few men are gripped by careers for the entire worklife, only a minority for as much as half the worklife."

environments, and thus more easily study person–environment interactions and their outcomes. The application of the theory to the life history is outlined in the following sections: "The Longitudinal Model," "Personal Development and Stability," "Vocational Behavior," "Academic Achievement," "Creative Performance," "Types and Personality Change."

THE LONGITUDINAL MODEL

The longitudinal model is a simple one: the person is conceived of as a personality type or personality pattern and assessed by his vocational preferences at various age levels (child, adolescent, and adult). His family, social group, school, college, and vocations are conceived of as environments and also assessed by vocational preferences. These two assumptions make it possible to predict many outcomes from the interactions shown in the model life history diagramed in Figure 2. This longitudinal formulation can be elaborated in many ways: by assigning single-digit codes to the person and each environment and then, on the basis of the formulations for the personality types and the environmental models, making predictions about interactions and outcomes; or by assigning two- to six-digit codes to each type and environment in the life span.

A person's movement from vocational preference to vocational preference, major field to major field, or occupation to occupation has been categorized in the following way. If, for a given time interval, a person maintains the same vocational preference or stays in the same major field or occupation, he is regarded as a "nonchanger" and coded 1.

If a person moves to a major field or an occupation in the same class as his original choice, he is called an "intraclass changer" and coded 2. Similar changes in vocational preferences are coded in the same way. For example, a student who first majors in physics and then switches to chemistry would be an "intraclass changer."

If a person moves from an occupation in one class to an occupa-

FIGURE 2

The Interactions of Persons and Environments

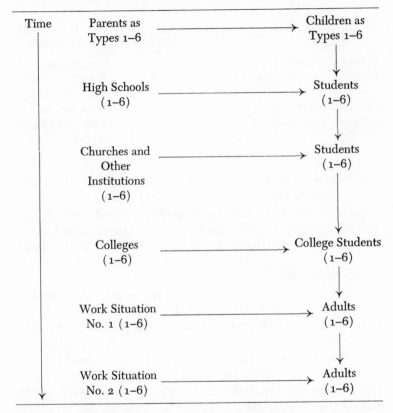

Time	Parents as Types 1–6	⟶	Children as Types 1–6
	High Schools (1–6)	⟶	Students (1–6)
	Churches and Other Institutions (1–6)	⟶	Students (1–6)
	Colleges (1–6)	⟶	College Students (1–6)
	Work Situation No. 1 (1–6)	⟶	Adults (1–6)
	Work Situation No. 2 (1–6)	⟶	Adults (1–6)

tion in a different class—for example, physicist to executive, artist to teacher, accountant to salesman—he is called an "interclass changer" and coded 3.

To determine intraclass and interclasss change, a person's preferences, major fields, or occupations are categorized in terms of the classification scheme given in Appendix A. This coding method makes it possible to give approximate weights to the degree of stability in a person's vocational preferences, educa-

TABLE 8

Some Examples of Changes in Vocation and Their Codes

Choice			
First	Second	Code No.	Description
Physicist to	Physicist	1	Nonchanger
Chemist to	Mathematician	2	Intraclass changer
Engineer to	Artist	3	Interclass changer
Social worker to	Accountant	3	Interclass changer
Salesman to	Sales manager	2	Intraclass changer
Teacher to	Salesman	3	Interclass changer

tional career, and work history. Moreover, because this method distinguishes between minor changes (for instance, from physicist to chemist, from mathematician to statistician) and major changes (for instance, from mathematician to musician, from biologist to administrator), it reduces the distortion inherent in the simple dichotomy of "change" versus "no change." Table 8 illustrates the coding procedures.

A preliminary study using this coding system lends support to the general hypothesis that students who leave a particular field of study in college lack some of the personal attributes—traits, aptitudes, self-concepts—associated with the typical student in his field of choice [72]. Strong's earlier work [121] and Cooley's recent longitudinal study [20] of high school and college students also support the hypothesis that incongruence between person and environment makes for instability. These studies give some support also to the hypothesis that a person remains in the field whose members he most resembles in his values, interests, self-concepts, and so on, although some of the findings were inconsistent. Related studies by Davis [28], Rosenberg [108], Pierson [102], and Warren [137] lend support to these results.

Because some people change jobs more often than once per unit of time (per year, for example), a more elaborate coding system for change is sometimes required. To take care of this situation, *intra*class changes can be coded 21–29; the second digit indicates the number of intraclass changes. *Inter*class changes can be coded 41–49: 41 represents one interclass change, 49 represents nine such changes. A code of 10 means there was no change in field. The gaps of 11 and 12 units between the three kinds of change are intended to maintain a minimal quantitative difference between no change, intraclass change, and interclass change. Table 9 illustrates this more complex coding scheme. Similar systems for assessing change can also be established by changing the weights for the various kinds of change.

In Table 9, Work History A is coded 10 because there was no change during the seven-year period. In History B, the first change is an *intra*class change, and so is coded 21; the second change—social worker to sales person—is an *inter*class change, and so is coded 41. Taken together, the changes in History B total 62. In History C, there was a total of five *intra*class changes, so the History is coded 25.

TABLE 9

A More Complex Coding Procedure for Work Histories

Time	Work Histories		
	A	B	C
0	Chemist	Elementary-school teacher	Car salesman
1 year		Social worker	Liquor salesman
2 years		Sales person	Insurance salesman
3 years			Small business owner
4 years			Insurance salesman
5 years			Real-estate salesman
6 years	↓	↓	↓
7 years	Chemist	Sales person	Real-estate salesman
Code	10	21 + 41 = 62	25

NOTE: When changes of several kinds occur, they can be coded and summed as in History B.

PERSONAL DEVELOPMENT AND STABILITY

It is assumed that a person's stability—personal and vocational —is determined chiefly by his personal development, particularly during his childhood. To be more specific, the stable person probably has parents whose individual personality patterns are consistent both in themselves and in relation to the other parent's personality pattern. Consequently, the parents' values and child-rearing practices are harmonious and free from conflict. These attributes foster consistent, integrated behavior in the child. Because the child perceives himself and the world accurately, he is more likely to select congruent environments for training and eventual vocation. This selection leads to achievement, satisfaction, and reinforcement of his particular coping behavior.

However, if one or both of the parents have inconsistent personality patterns, or if the father's pattern is inconsistent with the mother's, then the child is likely to develop inconsistent values, ineffective coping behavior, an inaccurate self-concept, and little self-confidence. Consequently, he will tend to vacillate, to make poor choices of environments, and to function ineffectively even in compatible environments.

In short, personal stability is the outcome of passing through a series of consistent environments that foster and strengthen one's ability to cope with the world in an integrated way. Instability, in contrast, results from living in a succession of inconsistent environments that create and perpetuate inaccurate, contradictory self-concepts and conflicting, ineffective coping behavior.

In Figure 3, the "Stable History" shows parents with consistent personality patterns. Their son has a consistent personality pattern, which is, in addition, related to his parents' personality patterns. The son selects jobs that are congruent with his personality pattern. The "Unstable History" in Figure 3 shows parents with inconsistent personality patterns and who are at war within themselves and with one another. These intrapersonal

FIGURE 3

Stable and Unstable Work Histories

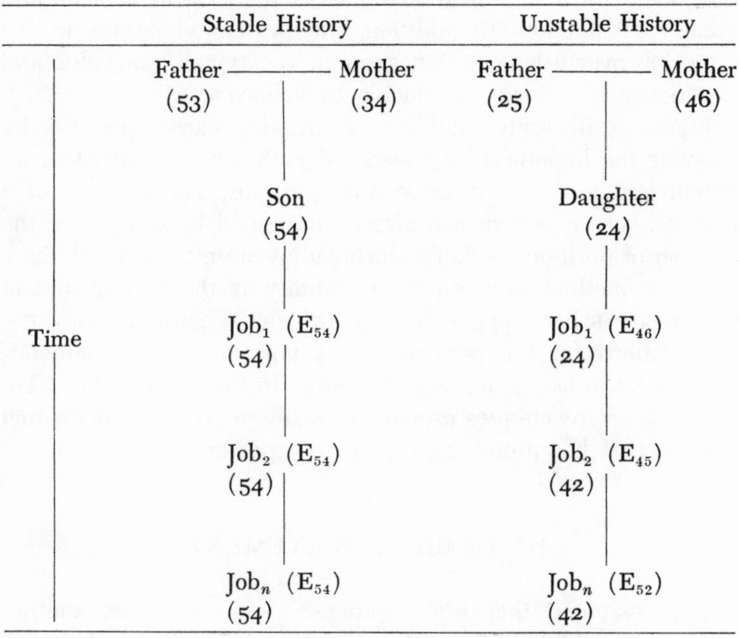

	Stable History		Unstable History	
	Father ——— Mother		Father ——— Mother	
	(53) (34)		(25) (46)	
	Son		Daughter	
	(54)		(24)	
Time	Job$_1$ (E$_{54}$)		Job$_1$ (E$_{46}$)	
	(54)		(24)	
	Job$_2$ (E$_{54}$)		Job$_2$ (E$_{45}$)	
	(54)		(42)	
	Job$_n$ (E$_{54}$)		Job$_n$ (E$_{52}$)	
	(54)		(42)	

NOTE: Numbers in parentheses are 2-digit codes for personality patterns and environmental models. Note that the stable history is associated with consistent codes and the unstable history with inconsistent codes.

and interpersonal relationships produce a daughter with a related but inconsistent personality pattern. The daughter selects several jobs in succession, none of which is congruent with her personality pattern.

VOCATIONAL BEHAVIOR

Looking at the longitudinal model, we can easily see that the stability or instability of the personality pattern may lead to certain kinds of behavior, which in turn produce such outcomes as vocational choice, stability, achievement, and satisfaction. For example, stable personal development leads to accurate self-knowledge and integrated coping behavior. These outcomes, in turn, make for better vocational choices, higher achievement, and greater satisfaction. In addition, the person who stays in the same job over a long period gains in vocational knowledge and experience—conditions conducive to achievement.

Figure 3 illustrates stable and unstable career patterns by showing the hypothesized vocational paths of persons with consistent and inconsistent personality patterns. The stability of a person's career pattern can also be examined by computing the number of positions he holds during a given unit of time. A more sensitive method of computing stability is the coding system described earlier (pages 82–83), which, because it uses the formulations for the personal types and model environments, permits us to assess *degrees* of change in the work history. Together, these techniques provide an easily interpreted conceptual scheme that has promising explanatory power.

ACADEMIC ACHIEVEMENT

It is assumed that high academic achievement is another product of a stable history. The dominance of Intellectual, Social, Artistic, and Conventional types in a person's personality pattern is conducive to success in academic work because such types have values, goals, and attitudes that are congruent with those of their teachers. Conversely, personality patterns dominated by Realistic and Enterprising types are less successful academically because of their relative incongruence with academic environments.

CREATIVE PERFORMANCE

Like academic achievement, creative performance is assumed to be a function of a stable and consistent life history. Given a stable history, the personality patterns of Intellectual-Artistic and

Artistic-Intellectual are most conducive to creative performance. This formulation may help to explain the commonsense notion that creativity is the result of "persistence" and "dedication." To elucidate: in the course of his development, the person with a consistent (that is, well-integrated) personality pattern develops well-defined, unified goals. Because he has eliminated extraneous and distracting subgoals he can discard those values, habits, and methods of coping that are irrelevant to his purpose and devote his effort to achieving his goal. Such a person is able to perform at a higher level than the person who is easily distracted by conflicting forces in himself or in his environment.

TYPES AND PERSONALITY CHANGE

So far, it has been assumed that vocational choice and other outcomes are the results of the interaction of immutable personality types in immutable environments. But, of course, people change. Traumatic events, such special experiences as psychotherapy, or simply the process of living and maturing—all of these factors foster changes that, presumably, lead the person to seek congruent environments. Moreover, environments change as their populations shift and alter. What is at one point a congruent environment for a particular person may become incongruent.

In the present theory, it is assumed that some types are more receptive to social experience and thus more prone to change than are others. The types listed in descending order in terms of their potential for change are Social, Enterprising, Conventional, Artistic, Intellectual, Realistic. Moreover, the person with an inconsistent pattern, because his values, needs, and abilities conflict and who therefore has a greater need of outside assistance, is especially sensitive to environmental pressures and is more likely to change. In contrast, the consistent personality has little need for assistance and is thus resistant to influence. For example, we would expect a person with a Social-Intellectual pattern to have great potential for change, whereas a person with a Realistic-Intellectual pattern would be unlikely to undergo personality change.

Similarly, environments change—because their populations change, because their members restructure the environment, or because outside influences act upon them. At this time, it is not possible to formulate exactly *how* such environmental and personal restructuring takes place.

SUMMARY

The extension of the theory to life patterns provides a way for conceptualizing personal development and the different outcomes associated with different patterns of development. Of equal importance, the longitudinal model suggests some of the conditions that lead to stable or unstable patterns.

The factors determining change in the person and in the environment are not altogether clear. Levinson's discussion [87] is useful in showing the complexity of the interaction of person and environment. More research and thought are needed before we can usefully apply the present theory to the life history.

CHAPTER EIGHT

Research and Practical
Applications

To MAKE THE THEORY outlined in this book more systematic and useful, extensive research is necessary. The formal statement of the theory should be reexamined logically to determine the adequacy of its definitions and classifications and to discover hypotheses that may have been overlooked in the present account. The hypotheses already suggested require extensive testing to determine their validity.

Those parts of the theory that were used to develop most of the hypotheses are of fundamental importance. The model types and environments, for instance, constitute the heart of the theory: their usefulness affects all the other parts. They represent only one of many possible typologies. Perhaps another classification scheme would prove more useful: schemes such as those suggested by Fine [39], Roe [104], or various factor analytic studies [4, 23, 37, 100, 127, 135] may be of greater value.

We need to explore more fully the problem of assessing the personality pattern. So far, the Vocational Preference Inventory and selected scales from the Strong Vocational Interest Blank have proved useful. But perhaps a simple personal history (which would capitalize on a wider range of information) would give a more accurate assessment. Whether or not the Personal Survey (Appendix B) fulfills our needs remains to be seen.

At this point the usefulness of the theory is only partially explored. The empirical studies that have been performed have been limited to investigating only a few of the hypotheses and have dealt with atypical samples [67, 68, 69, 71, 72, 110, 118]. We need many more comprehensive studies of the following aspects of the theory: (1) the personality types and their hypothetical attributes, (2) the model environments and their hypothetical attributes, (3) the life histories as revealed by personal histories and work histories, (4) the interaction of people and environments, especially studies of the same people over extended time intervals. The individual chapters suggest some starting points for these studies. Ideally, they should use large samples, the larger the better, because classifications by sex, type, and subtype reduce the subjects in any given category to a number so low that reliable statistical tests are not possible.

We need to study a greater variety of occupations simultaneously. Studies using the "closed system"—that is, studies such as Nachmann's [97] and Segal's [111], which are limited to single occupations or pairs of occupations—though suited to investigating special problems, leave much to be desired. They are difficult to execute because of prohibitive research costs, and they give us incomplete information that is hard to integrate with current knowledge. The present typology, on the other hand, provides an "open system," which, according to Clark [19], is more useful for organizing our present knowledge about interests.

We need to study more representative samples over longer time intervals. A large portion of the evidence for the present theory rests on atypical samples (exceptionally talented high school and college students) studied over relatively short periods. Whether or not the theory is applicable to people in lower-level occupations is a moot question.

The theory needs to be extended to account for learning and change. Hill [61] proposes that learning theory can be applied to the study of how people acquire values (and, by implication, interests), and that such processes as "identification," "introjection," and "internalization" can be analyzed, using terms drawn from learning theory. He outlines a reinforcement framework for such analyses and presents an analysis of the concept of conscience and the factors influencing its development. He argues that his scheme would simplify terminology, encourage more precise study, and further the integration of learning and personality theories. The present theory, like most theories of personality and vocational choice [70], has little to say about learning.

Finally, we must either make more efficient predictions on the basis of theory or abandon our efforts to construct theories. Despite several decades of research, the most efficient way to predict vocational choice is simply to ask the person what he wants to be; our best devices do not exceed the predictive value of that method [68, 94].

The theory may be valuable in dealing with a number of practical problems. The following suggestions, all of which stem from the present formulations, are offered for whatever heuristic values they may have for the professional personnel worker or clinical psychologist.

The theory provides a way of conceptualizing psychotherapy and counseling. In theoretical terms, psychotherapy can be viewed as the process of integrating people who have inconsistent (that is, unintegrated) personality patterns, by changing and resolving their developmental patterns. Personal and vocational counseling can be viewed as the process of helping persons to deal with themselves as they are and to find appropriate environments in which to live. It follows from this view that vocational counseling is most effective for people with consistent personality patterns.

The theory may be useful in training psychologists, vocational counselors, and personnel workers. It can be used to conceptualize the client, his history, and his future plans, thus providing the trainee with a framework for what would otherwise be a chaotic mass of information drawn from life histories, interviews, and test scores. For instance, with the major headings of the six formulations to guide him, the trainee can use the information drawn from diagnostic interviews and tests to categorize the client as one of the six types. Not only does this classification give order and shape to otherwise amorphous data, but it also indicates what additional information should be sought from the client. The client's occupational goals can be viewed in terms of the model environments; possible interactions can then be explored. Whatever the ultimate validity of the theory, it will, thus used, sharpen the trainee's perceptions of others.

For the practitioner, the theory provides a starting point for developing new classifications as well as a framework for organizing and interpreting studies of specific occupations and vocational choice, achievement, and creativity. Because the theory views vocational interests as an expression of personality, it enables the practitioner to integrate knowledge about vocational choice with other information about personality. For example, the practitioner may find it instructive to apply the type names to equivalent scales from interest inventories, following the equivalencies given in Table 2 page 37. In this way, more fruitful interpretations of otherwise isolated data can be made.

Similarly, the theory may be useful in selecting persons for scholarships, fellowships, and jobs. At present, such selections are usually done with no explicit rationale to serve as a guide. The present scheme, because it is explicit and systematic, could provide such a rationale.

The present models may also make possible the investigation of the nature of leadership and supervision. We would expect, for example, that the personality pattern of the head of an organization would provide a clue to the organization's growth and development, its policies and regulations, the kinds of personality types who survive in it, and the like. Presumably, by using the typology to assess the personality patterns of leaders and subordinates, we can predict the effectiveness of various pairings.

The value of the theory to the vocational counselor who works with normal adults is immediately apparent. Although there is no direct evidence that it will also be helpful to the counselor or psychologist working with psychiatric patients, it may well provide a valuable diagnostic framework.

The formulations for the types imply that people of different types have different reactions to psychotherapy. Realistic, Conventional, and Enterprising types would probably benefit less from psychotherapy than would Intellectual, Social, and Artistic types. The formulations also imply that different kinds of treatment are suitable for different types of people. Individual psychotherapy would be effective with the Social, Intellectual, and Artistic types, whereas somatic and activity therapies might be more effective with the Realistic, Conventional, and Enterprising types. One could use the present typology to analyze more exactly how successful a particular treatment is for a particular type. For example, the personality pattern of the therapist (who would constitute, in essence, a single-person environment) and the personality pattern of the patient could be coded, and then, on the basis of the person–environment interactions hypothesized earlier, predictions could be made. We would expect that congruent interactions would be conducive to learning, because congruence implies that the therapist and the patient share many attributes. The pairing of a therapist and a patient who differed to a moderate degree would be even more conducive to change, because it would produce a useful strain in the interpersonal relationship. Gross differences, however, would probably create barriers in communication and thus impede change.

A patient's reaction to trauma and illness and his subsequent rehabilitation might also be related to his personality type. For example, a man of the Realistic type would probably react very differently to a heart attack than would a man of the Artistic type. The Realistic man would be greatly concerned about continuing to play a man's role. If his cardiologist recommended that he change jobs, he would attempt to find a "masculine" position. He would probably have less insight into and less readiness to accept his heart disease and its consequences. In contrast, heart disease would be less threatening to the Artistic person, because masculinity is not a trait that is prominent in his self-image.

Using the Kuder Preference Record, Forer [41, 42] found evidence that suggests that certain physical illnesses and traumas are associated with certain personality types. The relation of illness to type seems to be consistent with speculation about the psychogenic nature of accident-proneness, heart disease, and alcoholism. At present, the evidence is suggestive only: more thorough and direct investigations of the connection between personality types and particular diseases are needed. For example, it might be useful to explore more fully the relationships between personality, smoking, and cancer.

The theory might usefully be applied to educational problems too. For example, a teacher could be assigned to a particular class on the basis of the congruence of his personality pattern with the profile of the class (estimated by the proportions of students of different types in the class). Such profiles could also be used to guide the teacher in choosing the most effective teaching methods and incentives to learning. Current attempts to interest engineering students in theoretical rather than practical problems might be more successful if appeals were couched in "Realistic" terms.

The formulations for the personality types provide a means for interpreting and perhaps predicting the behavior of social groups and organizations. For example, in the period immediately following Sputnik, the Engineering Council began publication of a periodical called *Action*—a title that seems consistent with the attributes of the Realistic type. To take another example: it is of interest that the labor movement has its greatest strength among the skilled trades and manual occupations (Realistic type) and that it has had relatively little success among occupations classified as Conventional and Enterprising. Various divisions of the American Psychological Association also behave in ways consistent with the formulations. For example, Division 17, Counseling Psychology, is assumed to consist of people who resemble primarily the Social type—a type that is, among other things, orally dependent. It is not surprising, then, that at annual meetings this group produces few research papers but contributes heavily to such socially oriented activities as symposia, conferences, and lectures. The recent movements of experimental psychologists to secede from the APA can also be explained by the theory. Because this group is assumed to consist of people who resemble the Intellectual type, one would expect that they would prefer to withdraw from the organization rather than to engage in constructive social interaction within the APA.

At this point, the research literature clearly suggests that vocational choice is the outcome of a person's developmental history, although the small, often negligible, statistical relationships between specific variables and vocational choice indicate that the forces that determine choice are complex and intricately interwoven. Apparently, a young person, by virtue of his heredity, family background, and school experience, learns to cope with some environmental tasks better than with others. With or without professional guidance, consciously or unconsciously, he perceives more or less accurately what he can do, what he cannot do, what he likes to do, and what he dislikes doing. Moreover, the young person acquires knowledge, more or less valid, about various occupations. On this basis he tentatively selects vocations that will, first, permit him to engage in activities and roles that are attractive to him and, second, enable him to avoid activities and roles that are distasteful or difficult.

These findings have several implications for the practice of vocational counseling. At present, the student's perceptions of various occupations are usually too broad and general; he needs to develop more differentiated images. For example, most students think of the term *researcher* as applying chiefly to the physicist or chemist, even though almost all occupations require researchers. Similarly, most students regard all teachers as underpaid, even though in actuality some teachers make very good money. If more differentiated images were developed, students might see themselves in more diverse vocations and roles *within* an occupation; this perception might serve to attract talented students into a wider variety of occupations. Occupational literature now tends to emphasize the most typical role within an occupation; it needs to be rewritten to emphasize the diversity of opportunities and roles within an occupation.

Since vocational choice is the outcome of a variety of influences, vocational counseling at the high school and college levels might be improved if students were given a chance to learn about different occupations through means other than just talking with a vocational counselor. For instance, the student might learn more about different vocations—and thereby make wiser vocational choices—if he were encouraged to work part time at different jobs or to talk with people actually employed in his field of interest. In short, it might be more useful if counseling center personnel were reduced and if psychologists and counselors concentrated on coordinating the interaction of students, special work and curriculum experiences, and employed adults rather than on directly advising the student. Also, because the evidence indicates that a person's past choices and tentative future choices are the most efficient and simple guides to his interests, counselors might make greater use of the client's expressed choices and reduce or abandon the use of interest inventories.

SUMMARY

Like most psychological theories, the present one will require extensive investigation to determine its general usefulness. At this time, several studies suggest that it has some value, but only after we have applied it to a greater range of populations and problems will we be able to evaluate its usefulness with any certainty. Similarly, its practical applications need to be extended and verified in a variety of settings: clinical, educational, and industrial.

References

1. ADLER, A. *Social Interest.* New York: Putnam, 1939.
2. ALLPORT, G. W. *Personality: A Psychological Interpretation.* New York: Holt, 1937.
3. ALLPORT, G. W., and P. E. Vernon. *A Study of Values.* Boston: Houghton Mifflin, 1931. (Revised ed. with P. E. Vernon and G. Lindzey, 1951.)
4. ASTIN, A. W. "Dimensions of Work Satisfaction in the Occupational Choices of College Freshmen." *Journal of Applied Psychology,* 1958, *42*, 187–190.
5. ASTIN, A. W. "An Empirical Characterization of Higher Educational Institutions." *Journal of Educational Psychology,* 1962, *53*, 224–235.
6. ASTIN, A. W. "Differential College Effects on the Motivation of Talented Students To Obtain the Ph.D." *Journal of Educational Psychology,* 1963, *54*, 63–71.
7. ASTIN, A. W. "Effects of Different College Environments on the Vocational Choices of High Aptitude Students." *Journal of Counseling Psychology,* 1965, *12*, 28–34.
8. ASTIN, A. W. "Further Validation of the Environmental Assessment Technique." *Journal of Educational Psychology,* 1963, *54*, 217–226.
9. ASTIN, A. W., and J. L. Holland. "The Environmental Assessment Technique: A Way To Measure College Environments." *Journal of Educational Psychology,* 1961, *52*, 308–316.
10. BARNETTE, W. L., Jr. "Occupational Aptitude Patterns of Selected Groups of Counseled Veterans." *Psychological Monographs,* 1961, *65* (Whole No. 322).

11. BEARDSLEE, D. C., and D. D. O'Dowd. "College Student Images of a Selected Group of Professions and Occupations." Wesleyan University, Middletown, Connecticut, 1960. (Mimeo)

12. BEILIN, H. "Discussion of the Super, Tiedeman, and Hall Papers." Paper read at the American Personnel and Guidance Association meetings, Chicago, 1962.

13. BERDIE, R. F. "Validities of the Strong Vocational Interest Blank." In W. L. Layton (Ed.), *The Strong Vocational Interest Blank: Research and Uses.* Minneapolis: University of Minnesota Press, 1960. Pp. 18–61.

14. BLAU, P. M., J. W. Gustad, R. Jessor, H. S. Parnes, and R. C. Wilcock. "Occupational Choice: A Conceptual Framework." *Industrial Labor Relations Review,* 1956, 9, 531–543.

15. BLOCK, J., and P. Petersen. "Q-Sort Item Analyses of a Number of Strong Vocational Interest Inventory Scales." OERL, AFPTRC, ARDC, 1955.

16. BORDIN, E. S. "A Theory of Interests As Dynamic Phenomena." *Educational and Psychological Measurement,* 1943, 3, 49–66.

17. BORDIN, E. S., Barbara Nachmann, and S. J. Segal. "An Articulated Framework for Vocational Development." *Journal of Counseling Psychology,* 1963, 10, 107–117.

18. BOYD, J. B. "Interests of Engineers Related to Turnover, Selection, and Management." *Journal of Applied Psychology,* 1961, 45, 143–149.

19. CLARK, K. E. *Vocational Interests of Nonprofessional Men.* Minneapolis: University of Minnesota Press, 1961.

20. COOLEY, W. W. "Career Development of Scientists." Cooperative Research Project No. 436, Office of Education, Graduate School of Education, Harvard University, 1963.

21. COTTLE, W. C. "A Factorial Study of the Multiphasic, Strong, Kuder, and Bell Inventories Using a Population of Adult Males." *Psychometrika,* 1950, 15, 25–47.

22. CRITES, J. O. "Ego-Strength in Relation to Vocational Interest Development." *Journal of Counseling Psychology,* 1960, 7, 137–143.

23. CRITES, J. O. "Factor Analytic Definitions of Vocational Motivation." *Journal of Applied Psychology,* 1961, 45, 330–337.

24. CRITES, J. O. *Vocational Psychology.* New York: McGraw-Hill, in press.

25. CRUTCHFIELD, R. S., D. G. Woodworth, and R. E. Albrecht.

"Perceptual Performance and the Effective Person." Lackland Air Force Base, Texas: Personnel Laboratory, Wright Air Development Center, April, 1958. (WADC–TN–58–60, ASTIA Document No. AD–151–039.)

26. DARLEY, J. G. "A Preliminary Study of Relations Between Attitude, Adjustment, and Vocational Interest Tests." *Journal of Educational Psychology*, 1938, *29*, 467–473.

27. DARLEY, J. G., and Theda Hagenah. *Vocational Interest Measurement.* Minneapolis: University of Minnesota Press, 1955.

28. DAVIS, J. A. "On the Congruence Between Occupational Values and Occupational Choice: A Panel Study of June, 1961, College Graduates." Paper read at American Psychological Association meetings, Philadelphia, August, 1963.

29. DAVIS, J. A. *Undergraduate Career Decisions.* Chicago: Aldine, 1964.

30. DAWIS, RENÉ V., G. W. England, and L. H. Lofquist. "A Theory of Work Adjustment." Minnesota Studies in Vocational Rehabilitation, *XV*, Bulletin 38, January, 1964.

31. DUNNETTE, M. D. "Vocational Interest Differences Among Engineers Employed in Different Functions." *Journal of Applied Psychology*, 1957, *41*, 273–278.

32. DUNNETTE, M. D., W. K. Kirchner, and JoAnne DeGidio. "Relations Among Scores on Edwards Personal Preference Schedule, California Psychological Inventory, and Strong Vocational Interest Blank for an Industrial Sample." *Journal of Applied Psychology*, 1958, *42*, 178–181.

33. DUNNETTE, M. D., P. Wernimont, and N. Abrahams. "Further Research in Vocational Interest Differences Among Several Types of Engineers." *Personnel and Guidance Journal*, 1964, *42*, 484–493.

34. EYSENCK, H. J. *The Scientific Study of Personality.* London: Routledge and Kegan Paul, 1952.

35. FAIRWEATHER, G. W., R. Simon, M. E. Gebhard, E. Weingarten, *et al.* "Relative Effectiveness of Psychotherapeutic Programs: A Multicriteria Comparison of Four Programs for Three Different Patient Groups." *Psychological Monographs*, 1960, *74*, No. 5 (Whole No. 492).

36. FERGUSON, L. W. "Ability, Interest and Aptitude." *Journal of Applied Psychology*, 1960, *44*, 126–131.

37. FERGUSON, L. W., L. G. Humphreys, and F. W. Strong. "A

Factorial Analysis of Interests and Values." *Journal of Educational Psychology*, 1941, *32*, 197–204.

38. FESTINGER, L. *A Theory of Cognitive Dissonance*. Evanston, Ill.: Peterson, 1957.

39. FINE, S. A. "The Structure of Worker Functions." *Personal and Guidance Journal*, 1955, *34*, 66–73.

40. FORER, B. R. "A Diagnostic Interest Blank." *Rorschach Research Exchange, and Journal of Projective Techniques*, 1948, *12*, 1–11.

41. FORER, B. R. "Personality Dynamics and Occupational Choice." Paper read at the American Psychological Association meetings, 1951.

42. FORER, B. R. "Personality Factors in Occupational Choice." *Educational and Psychological Measurement*, 1953, *13*, 361–366.

43. FORSYTH, R. P., and G. W. Fairweather. "Psychotherapeutic and Other Hospital Criteria: The Dilemma." *Journal of Abnormal and Social Psychology*, 1961, *62*, 598–604.

44. FRIEND, JEANNETTE G., and E. A. Haggard. "Work Adjustment in Relation to Family Background." *Psychological Monographs*, 1948, No. 16.

45. FROMM, E. *Man for Himself*. New York: Rinehart, 1947.

46. GALINSKY, M. D. "Personality Development and Vocational Choice of Clinical Psychologists and Physicists." *Journal of Counseling Psychology*, 1962, *9*, 299–305.

47. GARMAN, G. A., and L. Uhr. "An Anxiety Scale for the Strong Vocational Interest Inventory: Development, Cross-Validation and Subsequent Tests of Validity." *Journal of Applied Psychology*, 1958, *42*, 241–246.

48. GEE, HELEN H. "A Correlational Matrix for the Strong Vocational Interest Blank and the Edwards Personal Preference Schedule." Association of American Medical Colleges, Evanston, Illinois, 1957.

49. GEE, HELEN H. "Differential Characteristics of Student Bodies —Implications for the Study of Medicine." Paper read at the Conference on Selection and Educational Differentiations, May, 1959, Berkeley, California, sponsored by the Field Service Center and the Center for the Study of Higher Education.

50. GEHLMANN, F. "Objective Tests As Indicators of Personality and Temperament." Unpublished doctoral dissertation, University of Chicago, 1951.

51. GHEI, S. "Vocational Interests, Achievement and Satisfaction." *Journal of Counseling Psychology*, 1960, 7, 132–136.

52. GINZBERG, E., S. W. Ginzberg, S. Axelrad, and J. L. Herma, *Occupational Choice: An Approach to a General Theory*. New York: Columbia University Press, 1951.

53. GOUGH, H. G. *Manual for the California Psychological Inventory*. Palo Alto: Consulting Psychologists Press, 1957.

54. GOUGH, H. G., M. G. McKee, and R. J. Yandell. *Adjective Check List Analyses of a Number of Selected Psychometric and Assessment Variables*. Berkeley: University of California, Institute for Personality Assessment and Research, 1955.

55. GRIGG, A. E. "Childhood Experience with Parental Attitudes: A Test of Roe's Hypothesis." *Journal of Counseling Psychology*, 1959, 6, 153–156.

56. GRUNES, W. F. "Looking at Occupations." *Journal of Abnormal and Social Psychology*, 1957, 54, 86–92.

57. GUILFORD, J. P., P. R. Christensen, N. A. Bond, Jr., and M. A. Sutton. "A Factor Analysis Study of Human Interests." *Psychological Monographs*, 1954, 68, 4 (Whole No. 375).

58. HAHN, M. E. *Psychoevaluation: Adaptation–Distribution–Adjustment*. New York: McGraw-Hill, 1963.

59. HAHN, M. E., and M. S. MacLean. *Counseling Psychology*. New York: McGraw-Hill, 1955.

60. HATHAWAY, S. R., E. D. Monachesi, and L. A. Young. "Rural–Urban Adolescent Personality." *Rural Sociology*, 1959, 24, 331–346.

61. HILL, W. F. "Learning Theory and the Acquisition of Values." *Psychological Review*, 1960, 67, 317–331.

62. HOLLAND, J. L. *Manual for the Vocational Preference Inventory*. Palo Alto: Consulting Psychologists Press, 1958. Now published by Educational Research Associates, Iowa City, Iowa.

63. HOLLAND, J. L. "A Personality Inventory Employing Occupational Titles." *Journal of Applied Psychology*, 1958, 42, 336–342.

64. HOLLAND, J. L. "A Theory of Vocational Choice." *Journal of Counseling Psychology*, 1959, 6, 35–45.

65. HOLLAND, J. L. "A Classification for Occupations in Terms of Personality and Intelligence." *American Psychologist*, 1959, 14, 476. (Abstract)

66. HOLLAND, J. L. "The Meaning of Interests." Paper presented at

the American Personnel and Guidance Association meetings, Chicago, March, 1962.

67. HOLLAND, J. L. "Some Explorations of a Theory of Vocational Choice: I. One- and Two-Year Longitudinal Studies." *Psychological Monographs*, 1962, *76*, 26 (Whole No. 545).

68. HOLLAND, J. L. "Some Explorations of a Theory of Vocational Choice and Achievement: II. A Four-Year Prediction Study." *Psychological Reports*, 1963, *12*, 545–594. Southern Universities Press, 1963 Monograph Supplement 4–V12.

69. HOLLAND, J. L. "Explorations of a Theory of Vocational Choice: IV. Vocational Preferences and Their Relation to Occupational Images, Daydreams and Personality." *Vocational Guidance Quarterly*, published in four parts in Summer, Autumn, and Winter issues. 1963–64.

70. HOLLAND, J. L. "Major Programs of Research on Vocational Behavior." In H. Borow (Ed.), *Man in a World of Work*. New York: Houghton Mifflin, 1964. Chapter 12.

71. HOLLAND, J. L. *Explorations of a Theory of Vocational Choice: V. A One-Year Prediction Study*. Moravia, N.Y.: Chronical Guidance Professional Service, 1964.

72. HOLLAND, J. L., and R. C. Nichols. "Explorations of a Theory of Vocational Choice: III. A Longitudinal Study of Change in Major Field of Study." *Personnel and Guidance Journal*, 1964, *43*, 235–242.

73. HOLLAND, J. L., and R. C. Nichols. "The Development and Validation of an Indecision Scale: The Natural History of a Problem in Basic Research." *Journal of Counseling Psychology*, 1964, *11*, 27–34.

74. JUNG, C. G. *Psychological Types*. New York: Harcourt, Brace, 1933.

75. KELLY, E. L., and D. W. Fiske. The *Prediction of Performance in Clinical Psychology*. Ann Arbor: University of Michigan Press, 1951.

76. KELLY, E. L., and L. R. Goldberg. "Correlates of Later Performance and Specialization in Psychology." *Psychological Monographs*, 1959, *73*, 12 (Whole No. 482).

77. KILBRICK, ANNE, and D. V. Tiedeman. "Conceptions of Self and Perception of Role in Relation to Continuation in Schools of Nursing." *Journal of Counseling Psychology*, 1961, *8*, 62–69.

78. KING, B. T. "Personality Correlates of Susceptibility to Influence

by Communications of Majority Opinion." Paper read at American Psychological Association meetings, Washington, 1958.

79. KORN, H. A. "Differences Between Majors in Engineering and Physical Sciences on CPI and SVIB Scores." *Journal of Counseling Psychology*, 1962, 9, 306–312.

80. KRETSCHMER, E. *Physique and Character*. New York: Harcourt, Brace, 1925. Berlin: Springer, 1921.

81. KRIEDT, P. H. "Vocational Interests of Psychologists." *Journal of Applied Psychology*, 1949, 33, 482–488.

82. KRULEE, G. K., and E. B. Nadler. "Studies of Education for Science and Engineering: Student Values and Curriculum Choice." IRE Transactions in Engineering Management, 1960, EM–7, 146–158.

83. KUBIE, L. S. "Some Unsolved Problems of the Scientific Career." *American Scientist*, 1954, 42, 104–112.

84. KUDER, G. F. "Administrator's Manual." Kuder Preference Record, Vocational, Form C, 1960. Science Research Associates, Chicago, Illinois.

85. LAURENT, H., Jr. A Study of the Developmental Backgrounds of Men To Determine by Means of the Biographical Information Blank the Relationship Between Factors in Their Early Backgrounds and Their Choice of Professions. Unpublished doctoral dissertation, Western Reserve University, 1951.

86. LECKY, P. *Self-Consistency*. New York: Island Press, 1945.

87. LEVINSON, D. J. "Role, Personality, and Social Structure in the Organizational Setting." *Journal of Abnormal and Social Psychology*, 1959, 58, 170–180.

88. LIBO, L. *The Cohesiveness of Groups*. Ann Arbor, Michigan: Research Center for Group Dynamics, 1953.

89. LINTON, R. *The Cultural Background of Personality*. New York, Century, 1945.

90. LOPEZ, F. M., Jr. "A Psychological Analysis of the Relationship of Role Consensus and Personality Consensus to Job Satisfaction and Job Performance." Unpublished doctoral dissertation, Columbia University, 1962.

91. LOWE, C. M. "The Self-Concept: Fact or Artifact?" *Psychological Bulletin*, 1961, 58, 325–336.

92. MACKINNON, D. W. "An Assessment Study of Air Force Officers." ASTIA Document No. AD–210–220. Personnel Laboratory, Lackland Air Force Base, Texas, 1958.

93. MacKinnon, D. W. "What Do We Mean by Talent and How Do We Test for It?" In *The Search for Talent: College Admissions 7*. New York: College Entrance Examination Board, 1960.

94. McArthur, C., and Lucia B. Stevens. "The Validation of Expressed Interests As Compared with Inventoried Interests: A Fourteen-Year Follow-up." *Journal of Applied Psychology*, 1955, 39, 184–189.

95. Mierzwa, J. A. "Comparison of Systems of Data for Predicting Career Choice." *Personnel and Guidance Journal*, 1963, 41, 29–34.

96. Murray, H. A. *Explorations in Personality*. New York: Oxford, 1938.

97. Nachmann, Barbara. "Childhood Experience and Vocational Choice in Law, Dentistry and Social Work." *Journal of Counseling Psychology*, 1960, 7, 243–250.

98. Nadler, E. B., and G. K. Krulee. "Personality Factors Among Science and Technology Freshmen." *Journal of Educational Psychology*, 1961, 52, 223–231.

99. Pace, C. R., and G. G. Stern. "An Approach to the Measurement of Psychological Characteristics of College Environments." *Journal of Educational Psychology*, 1958, 49, 269–277.

100. Palmer, G. J., Jr., and E. J. McCormick. "A Factor Analysis of Job Activities." *Journal of Applied Psychology*, 1961, 45, 289–294.

101. Patterson, C. H. "Interest Tests and the Emotionally Disturbed Client." *Educational and Psychological Measurement*, 1957, 17, 264–280.

102. Pierson, R. R. "Changes of Majors by University Students." *Personnel and Guidance Journal*, 1962, 41, 458–461.

103. Reid, J. W., A. P. Johnson, F. N. Entwisle, and W. P. Angers. "A Four-Year Study of the Characteristics of Engineering Students." *Personnel and Guidance Journal*, 1962, 40, 38–43.

104. Roe, Anne. "A New Classification of Occupations." *Journal of Counseling Psychology*, 1954, 1, 215–220.

105. Roe, Anne. *The Psychology of Occupations*. New York: Wiley, 1956.

106. Roe, Anne. "Early Determinants of Vocational Choice." *Journal of Counseling Psychology*, 1957, 4, 212–217.

107. Roe, Anne, and M. Siegelman. *A Study of the Origin of Interests*.

APGA Inquiry Studies—No. 1, Washington, D.C.: American Personnel and Guidance Association, 1964.

108. ROSENBERG, M. *Occupations and Values.* Glencoe, Ill.: Free Press, 1957.

109. SANFORD, N. (Ed.). *The American College.* New York: Wiley, 1962.

110. SCHUTZ, R. A., and D. H. Blocher. "Self-Satisfaction and Level of Occupational Choice." *Personnel and Guidance Journal,* 1961, *40,* 595–598.

111. SEGAL, S. I. "The Role of Personality Factors in Vocational Choice: A Study of Accountants and Writers." Unpublished doctoral dissertation, University of Michigan, 1953.

112. SHELDON, W. H. (with the collaboration of C. W. Dupertuis and E. McDermott). *Atlas of Men: A Guide for Somatotyping the Adult Male at All Ages.* New York: Harper, 1954.

113. SHELDON, W. H. *The Varieties of Temperament.* New York: Harper, 1942.

114. SPRANGER, E. *Types of Men.* Translated from 5th German edition of *Lebensformen* by Paul J. W. Pigors. Halle: Max Niemeyer Verlag, 1928.

115. STERN, G. G., M. I. Stein, and B. S. Bloom. *Methods in Personality Assessment.* Glencoe, Ill.: Free Press, 1956.

116. STERNBERG, C. "Interests and Tendencies Toward Maladjustment in a Normal Population." *Personnel and Guidance Journal,* 1956, *35,* 94–99.

117. STEWART, L. H. "Mother-Son Identification and Vocational Interest." *Genetic Psychology Monographs,* 1959, *60,* 31–63.

118. STOCKIN, B. C. "A Test of Holland's Occupational Level Formulation." *Personnel and Guidance Journal,* 1964, *54,* 599–602.

119. STONE, V. W. "Measured Interests in Relation to Intraoccupational Proficiency." *Journal of Applied Psychology,* 1960, *44,* 78–82.

120. STOTLAND, E. "Determinants of Attraction to Groups." *Journal of Social Psychology,* 1959, *49,* 71–80.

121. STRONG, E. K., Jr. *Vocational Interests of Men and Women.* Stanford: Stanford University Press, 1943.

122. STRONG, E. K., Jr., and A. C. Tucker. "The Use of Vocational Interest Scales in Planning a Medical Career." *Psychological Monographs,* 1952, *66,* 9 (Whole No. 341).

123. SUPER, D. E., and P. B. Bachrach. *Scientific Careers and Voca-*

tional Development Theory. New York: Teachers College, Columbia University, Bureau of Publications, 1957.

124. SUPER, D. E., and J. O. Crites. *Appraising Vocational Fitness.* New York: Harper, 1962.

125. SUPER, D. E., J. O. Crites, R. C. Hummel, H. P. Moser, *et al. Vocational Development.* New York: Teachers College, Columbia University, Bureau of Publications, 1957.

126. SUPER, D. E., R. Starishevsky, N. Matlin, and J. P. Jordaan. *Career Development: Self-Concept Theory.* New York: College Entrance Examination Board, 1963.

127. TERWILLIGER, J. S. "Dimensions of Occupational Preference." *Educational and Psychological Measurement,* 1963, *23,* 525–542.

128. THORNDIKE, R. L., and Elizabeth Hagen. *10,000 Careers.* New York: Wiley, 1959.

129. TIEDEMAN, D. V., and R. P. O'Hara. *Career Development: Choice and Adjustment.* New York: College Entrance Examination Board, 1963.

130. TYLER, LEONA E. "The Relationship of Interests to Abilities and Reputation Among First Grade Children." *Educational and Psychological Measurement,* 1951, *11,* 255–264.

131. TYLER, LEONA E. "Research Explorations in the Realm of Choice." *Journal of Counseling Psychology,* 1961, *8,* 195–201.

132. UNITED STATES EMPLOYMENT SERVICE. Estimates of worker trait requirements for 4000 jobs. United States Department of Labor, Bureau of Employment Security, U.S.E.S. Washington, D.C.: U.S. Government Printing Office, 1958.

133. UTTON, A. C. "Recalled Parent-Child Relations As Determinants of Vocational Choice." *Journal of Counseling Psychology,* 1962, *9,* 49–53.

134. VANCE, F. L., and T. C. Volsky, Jr. "Counseling and Psychotherapy: Split Personality or Siamese Twins." *American Psychologist,* 1962, *17,* 565–570.

135. VERNON, P. E. "Classifying High-Grade Occupational Interests." *Journal of Abnormal and Social Psychology,* 1949, *44,* 85–96.

136. VRIS, R., and P. H. Kriedt. "Predicting Employee Turnover with Measures of Interest and Response Set." Paper presented at the Eastern Psychological Association meetings, Philadelphia, 1961.

137. WARREN, J. R. "Self-Concept, Occupational Role Expectation,

and Change in College Major." *Journal of Counseling Psychology*, 1961, *8*, 164–169.

138. WEISSMAN, M. P. "An Approach to the Assessment of Intellectual Disposition Among Selected High-Ability Students." Unpublished doctoral dissertation, University of California, 1958.

139. WILENSKY, H. "Orderly Careers and Social Participation." *American Sociological Review*, 1961, *26*, 521–539.

140. WOODWORTH, D. G., J. Block, and D. W. MacKinnon. "A Comparison of Data Derived from Q-Sorts and Rating Scales." Research Report, OERL, AFPTRC, ARDC, May, 1955.

Appendix A

A CLASSIFICATION SCHEME
FOR DETERMINING A PERSON'S RESEMBLANCE
TO THE MODEL TYPES

THE FOLLOWING LISTS of occupational titles and major fields were prepared as criteria for use in exploring a theory of vocational choice. The lists can be used to classify expressed vocational choices, choices of major field, changes in such preferences, and work histories (movement within a class or from class to class over some specified time interval).

Part I contains the most comprehensive criteria for classifying occupations; it includes occupational titles used as items in the third, fourth, and fifth revisions of the VPI, plus other occupations. Part II contains only those occupations included in the fourth revision of the VPI. And Table 1, page 16 contains only the items in the fifth revision of the VPI. All three classifications result in similar categorization. They differ principally in their comprehensiveness.

For research, the most homogeneous scheme (the one given in Table 1) is the most useful. When in doubt about what class a given occupation belongs in, it is better to omit the occupation, because "errors" in classification probably reduce expected relationships.

Part II contains lists of occupational titles for determining a person's resemblance to the types and some subtypes. These items are from the fourth revision of the VPI. Subtypes were found by inspecting the correlations between each occupational title and the six scales—Realistic, Intellectual, Social, Conventional, Enterprising, and Artistic—for a group of 400 male National Merit Finalists.

If an item has its highest correlation with the Realistic scale and its next highest correlation with the Intellectual scale, it is coded as a subtype, 12. Ties are indicated by underlining (_____).

The usefulness of these subtypes is not known at present. A person's preferences for the occupations associated with each subtype can be scored so that his resemblance to each subtype can be estimated. The rationale for the types in Chapter 2 can be used to predict outcomes. Whether or not this technique is preferable to using coded VPI scales or the Personal Survey remains to be determined.

Part I

COMPREHENSIVE CLASSIFICATIONS FOR VOCATIONAL CHOICES AND OCCUPATIONS

1. Realistic Occupations

Laborers and Skilled Tradesmen
    Cook
    Construction worker
    Electrician, carpenter, master plumber
    Electronic technicians (TV station, laboratory, etc.)
    Filling station attendant
    Inspector of construction, livestock, machines, etc.
    Janitor
    Machinist
    Mechanic (automobile, airplane)
    Radio operator
    Repairman (TV and radio, piano, furniture, etc.)
    Tool designer, tool and die maker

Vehicle Drivers (truck driver, locomotive engineer, aviator, bus driver, heavy equipment driver)

Agriculture and Livestock Workers (farmer, rancher, hunter-trapper)

Natural Resource Conservationists (forest ranger, fish and wildlife specialist, soil expert)

Servicemen (enlisted men and officers except chaplains 3, medical doctors 3)

Engineers (all except sales engineer 5) (chemical, electrical, mechanical, civil, industrial, metallurgical, marine, etc.)

College Teachers Of
Engineering and engineering physics
Agriculture
Mining
Animal husbandry

Miscellaneous
Draftsman (engineering, maps, etc.)
Surveyor
Weather observer
Detective, FBI agent
Mail carrier
Policeman, fireman
Laboratory technician (not medical technologist or tester)

2. Intellectual Occupations

Physical and Biological Scientists (astronomer, atomic scientist, chemist, geologist, meteorologist, physicist, biologist, botanist, naturalist, zoologist)

Related Scientists
Anthropologist
Archeologist
Architect
Computer design and programer
Dentist
Experimental psychologist
Inventor

Mathematician (mathematics in business or industry 4)
Philosopher
Scientific research worker
Statistician
Veterinarian
Medical technologist
Medical researcher

Science Writers
Writer of scientific articles
Editor of scientific journal
Science-fiction writer

College Teachers Of
Physical and biological sciences
Research science
Experimental psychology
Mathematics
Philosophy
Premedical (girls *only*, boys are 3)
Predental
Computer design and programing
Astrophysics

3. Social Occupations

Religious Workers
Minister, foreign missionary (including medical missionary)
Chaplain in armed services

Social Service and Welfare Workers
Grade-school teachers
Guidance counselor, therapist (marriage or vocational counselor, speech therapist, psychiatrist—M & F, clinical psychologist)
High school teacher (by field, physical education teacher too)
Juvenile delinquency expert
Medical doctors (all specialties including ophthalmologist, oculist, and nonmedical optometrist, if research is specified, 2) (girls are 2)
Nurse
Playground director

Salvation Army officer
School principal and superintendent of education, schools, etc.
Social worker
YMCA secretary, Boy Scout official, director of welfare agency

College Teachers Of
Theology
Premedical (boys *only,* girls are 2)
Home economics, dietetics
Education
Sociology
Psychology (except experimental 2)
Nursing
Speech therapy, speech correction

Miscellaneous
College teacher when field is not specified
Conciliator (employee-employer)
Employment interviewer
Judge
Psychologist when field is not specified
Public health officer
Truant officer (education)

4. Conventional Occupations

Financial Workers
Accountant (certified public accountant, actuary, auditor, book-
keeper)
All bank employees except officials
Budget reviewer, financial analyst
Cashier
Cost estimator, cost engineer
Credit investigator
Rate analyst
Secretary-treasurer of firms
Tax expert, Internal Revenue agent

Office Workers
Clerk (post office, payroll, shipping and receiving, etc.)
IBM equipment operator

Office manager
Secretary and assistants (administrative, executive, legal, etc.)
Traffic manager

College Teachers Of
Accounting
Banking
Business (*not* administration or management 5)
Commerce and finance
Economics

Miscellaneous
Customs liquidator
Efficiency expert
Inventory controller
Quality control
Records supervisor
Real-estate appraiser
Statistician (*except* where theoretical or nonapplied statistician is
specified 2)
Proofreader
Adjudicator
Supply officer

5. Enterprising Occupations

Sales Personnel (buyer, distributor)
Salesman, manufacturer's representative, store clerk, auctioneer (of
products), seller of real estate, insurance, stocks and bonds, etc.

Owners and Managers of a Business, Including
Contractor
Importer
Investment, finance business, speculator
Publisher (newspaper, book)
Business or sports promoter
Advertising man
Optician (see 3 on other "eye" professions)
Travel consultant
(*Not* pharmacist)

Managers and Supervisors
Business executive and manager (*not* secretary-treasurer 4)
Sales manager, sales engineer
Foreman, supervisor of production and other men (*not* machines 1)
Directors (of research and development laboratories, etc.)
(*Not* office manager 4)
Lawyers (attorney, counsel or private or corporation, *not* judges 3)

College Teachers Of
Business administration and management (*only,* see 4)
International relations (foreign service programs)
Political science and government
Prelaw, Law
History

Miscellaneous
Master of ceremonies
Politician (congressional lobbyist, political campaign manager, state governor)
Radio-TV program director, announcer, producer
College president or dean
Diplomat, foreign service officer, United Nations officer (*not* secretary 4, translator 6)
Personnel manager
Labor relations man (industrial relations)
Insurance claims adjustor
Industrial psychologist

6. *Artistic Occupations*

Creative Artists
Writer, editor (novelist, journalist, newspaper reporter, advertising copy writer)
Artist, designer, decorator (portrait artist, furniture or clothing designer, window decorator, interior decorator, advertising layout man)
Theatrical artists (actor, stage director)
Musician (arranger, composer, pop singer, etc.)

College Teachers Of
English
Theater, dramatics

Art
Music
Journalism
Speech (general)

Miscellaneous
Art and music critic
Art dealer
Cartoonist
Humorist
Linguist, translator, interpreter

TYPICAL UNCLASSIFIABLE OCCUPATIONS

Pharmacist
Professional student
Tramp
Playboy
Unspecified civil service or government work

Part II

EXPERIMENTAL CLASSIFICATION FOR VOCATIONAL CHOICES AND OCCUPATIONS*

1. Realistic Occupations

(CODE 12)	(CODE 14)
Surveyor (.83)	Power station operator (.83)
Tool designer (.79)	Radio operator (.83)

* If an item had its highest correlation with the Realistic Scale and its next highest correlation with the Intellectual Scale, it was coded as a subtype 12. Ties are indicated by underlining (_____). Correlations in parentheses indicate the correlation between the occupational title and the VPI scale with which it is most highly correlated.

(CODE 12)

Electrician (.79)
Photoengraver (.78)
Blaster (dynamiter) (.71)
Tree surgeon (.70)
Aviator (.66)
Fish and wildlife specialist (.62)
Forest ranger (.62)
Test pilot (.61)
Draftsman (.59)
Hunter and trapper (.59)
Weather observer (.57)
North woods guide (.55)
Deep-sea diver (.52)
Wild-animal trainer (.52)
Lighthouse keeper (.46)
Explorer (.45)
Mountain climber (.42)
Truck gardener (.37)

(CODE 14)

Crane operator (.79)
Power shovel operator (.79)
Machinist (.78)
Locksmith (.76)
Airplane mechanic (.75)
Auto mechanic (.73)
Locomotive engineer (.73)
Master plumber (.67)
Filling station attendant (.62)
Factory foreman (.58)
Truck driver (.58)
Air force ace (.55)
Barber (.51)

(CODE 15)

Carpenter (.73)
Wrecker (building) (.68)
Railroad conductor (.61)
Fireman (.60)
Ranch hand (cowboy) (.56)
Racing car driver (.55)
Photographer (.55)
Jockey (.53)
Stunt man (motion picture) (.52)
Motorcycle driver (.51)
Narcotics inspector (.43)
Detective (.42)
FBI agent (.37)
Prize fighter (.34)
Professional football player (.29)

(CODE 16)

Hypnotist (.28)

12. Realistic-Intellectual Occupations

Electronic technician (.66, .66)
Engineer (.62, .60)

14. Realistic-Conventional Occupation

Construction inspector (.76)

2. Intellectual Occupations

(CODE 21)

Zoologist (.82)
Botanist (.79)
Aeronautic design engineer (.78)
Geologist (.76)
Astronomer (.75)
Writer of scientific or technical
 articles (.75)
Biologist (.74)
Experimental laboratory engineer
 (.74)
Chemist (.73)
Scientific research worker (.73)
Interplanetary scientist (.73)
Physicist (.72)
Bacteriologist (.71)
Meteorologist (.71)
Atomic scientist (.70)
Independent research scientist (.70)
Mathematician (.62)
Medical laboratory technician (.62)
Scientific theorist (.61)
Archeologist (.58)
Inventor (.56)
Scientific authority (.51)

(CODE 26)

Anthropologist (.81)
Editor of scientific journal (.75)

(CODE 23)

Surgeon (.46)

3. Social Occupations

(CODE 35)

Personal counselor (.83)
Vocational counselor (.82)
Conciliator (employee–employer relations) (.77)
Assistant City School Superintendent (.69)
Playground director (.66)
Parole officer (.64)
Employment interviewer (.64)
Truant officer (.62)
UN official (.60)
Physical education teacher (.53)
Boy Scout official (.45)

(CODE 35)

Athletic coach (.39)
Police judge (.35)
Ward attendant (.35)

(CODE 36)

Psychiatric case worker (.82)
Social science teacher (.78)
Rehabilitation worker (.75)
Speech therapist (.70)
Social worker (.67)
High school teacher (.66)
Clinical psychologist (.64)
Foreign missionary (.63)
Elementary-school teacher (.62)
Psychiatrist (.58)
College professor (.53)

(CODE 36)

Florist (.40)
English teacher (.36)

(CODE 365)

Juvenile delinquency expert (.81)
Marriage counselor (.76)
School principal (.71)
Director of welfare agency (.71)
World peace organizer (.59)

(CODE 356)

Criminal psychologist (.57)
Funeral director (.46)

(CODE 345)

YMCA secretary (.44, .44, .41)

(CODE 362)

Experimental psychologist (.47)

(CODE 32)

Public health official (.58)
Medical illustrator (.58)
Pediatrician (.56)
Physician (.42)

4. Conventional Occupations

(CODE 45)

Financial analyst (.81)
Tax expert (.79)
Traffic manager (.78)
Bank examiner (.77)
Cost estimator (.75)
Inventory controller (.68)
Administrative secretary (.66)
Budget reviewer (.63)
Cashier (.61)
C.P.A. (.59)
Bookkeeper (.58)
Insurance clerk (.41)

(CODE 45)

Office manager (.78)
Real-estate appraiser (.69)
Administrative assistant (.67)
Production manager (.63)
Credit investigator (.61)
Chief clerk (.61)
International trade economist (.51)

(CODE 41)

Quality control expert (.66)
Bank teller (.62)
Payroll clerk (.55)
Post office clerk (.46)

(CODE 415, 412)

IBM equipment operator (.66)
Shipping and receiving clerk
 (.54)
Policeman (.52)

(CODE 425)

Statistician (.67)
Records supervisor (.65)
Efficiency expert (.58)

(CODE 435)

Court stenographer (.53)

5. Enterprising Occupations

(CODE 54)

Business executive (.89)
Hotel manager (.81)
Manufacturer's representative (.80)
Political campaign manager (.77)
Master of ceremonies (.76)

(CODE 53)

Industrial relations consultant
 (.77)
Congressional lobbyist (.68)
Travel consultant (.62)
Supreme court judge (.58)

(CODE 54)

President of manufacturing company (.75)
Business promoter (.74)
Transcontinental railroad president (.74)
Sales manager (.74)
Sales engineer (.72)
Stock and bond salesman (.70)
Buyer (.70)
Traveling salesman (.67)
Real-estate salesman (.65)
Speculator (.63)
Life insurance salesman (.62)
Internal Revenue collector (.59)
Army general (.46)
Professional athlete (.31)

(CODE 54)

Insurance manager (.70)
Banker (.69)
Stockbroker (.67)
Headwaiter (.61)
Route salesman (.44)
Army officer (.41)

(CODE 56)

TV producer (.83)
Radio announcer (.62)

(CODE 53)

Public relations man (.75)
Personnel manager (.66)
Congressional investigator (.60)
Diplomat (.57)
Prosecuting attorney (.55)
Judge (.55)
Criminal lawyer (.54)
Lawyer (.48)
University president (.47)
Criminologist (.46)

(CODE 51)

Sports promoter (.61)
Restaurant worker (.50)
Referee (sporting events) (.46)

(CODE 51)

Liquor salesman (.57)
Private investigator (.46)
Treasury agent (.46)
Counter-Intelligence man (.41)
Gambling dealer (.33)

6. Artistic Occupations

(CODE 63)

Composer (.86)
Playwright (.85)
Music critic (.84)
Art dealer (.82)
Art critic (.81)

(CODE 65)

Stage director (.72)
Cartoonist (.69)
Dance band leader (.64)
Newspaper reporter (.64)
Interior decorator (.58)

(CODE 63)

Dramatic coach (.81)
Symphony conductor (.80)
Free-lance writer (.79)
Concert singer (.78)
Musical arranger (.77)
Actor (.73)
Musician (.73)
Novelist (.72)
Sculptor (.72)
Author (.71)
Poet (.70)
Commercial artist (.70)
Portrait artist (.67)
Stage designer (.66)
Clothing designer (.64)
Humorist (.59)

(CODE 65)

Book censor (.44)

(CODE 635)

Newspaper editor (.49)

Part III

CRITERION LISTS FOR FIELDS OF STUDY

1. Realistic (Revision)

Agriculture†
Agricultural education
Industrial arts†
Engineering‡
Forestry†
Trade and industry
Animal husbandry†
Mining

EAT Majors*

Agriculture
Agricultural education
Physical education
Recreation
Industrial arts
Engineering
Forestry
Trade and industry

2. Intellectual

Architecture
Biological sciences†
Geography

EAT Majors*

Architecture
Biological sciences
Geography

2. *Intellectual*

Medical technology†
Mathematics†
Philosophy
Physical sciences†
Anthropology
Experimental psychology
Premedical (girls only)
Research engineering†

EAT Majors°

Medical technology
Pharmacy
Mathematics
Philosophy
Physical sciences
Anthropology

3. *Social*

Health education
Education of exceptional children
   and mentally retarded†
Speech correction
Education (unclassified)†
Nursing
Occupational therapy†
Physical therapy
Scholastic philosophy
Social science (general)
American civilization
Sociology
Social work†
Premedical (boys only)
Home economics
Dietetics
Physical education
Recreation
Theology†
Psychology (except experimental)†

EAT Majors°

Health education
Education of exceptional children
   and mentally retarded
Speech correction
Education (unclassified)
Nursing
Occupational therapy
Physical therapy
Scholastic philosophy
Social science (general)
American civilization
Sociology
Social work

4. *Conventional (Revision)*

Accounting†
Secretarial
Business and commercial°°
   (general and unclass.)
Business education
Economics†
Finance†

EAT Majors°

Accounting
Secretarial
Business and commercial
   (general and unclass.)
Business education
Library science

5. *Enterprising*

Hotel and restauraunt administration†
Hospital administration†
History
International relations
Political science
Foreign service
Industrial relations
Public administration†
Prelaw
Sales engineering
Business administration and management†

*EAT Majors**

Hotel and restaurant administration
Hospital administration
History
International relations
Political science
Foreign service
Industrial relations
Public administration

6. *Artistic*

Art education
Music education
English and journalism
Fine and applied arts (all fields)
Foreign language and literature (all fields)
Speech (except speech correction and therapy)

*EAT Majors**

Art education
Music education
English and journalism
Fine and applied arts (all fields)
Foreign language and literature (all fields)

Unclassifiable College Majors

1. Double majors falling in different classes (that is, engineering and accounting, mathematics and education).

2. Ambiguous majors (that is, rocketry, aviation, social relations, etc.)

* Used by Astin and Holland [9].
† The major fields that are most typical of a given type.
‡ Except sales and research engineering.
** Not administrative or management.

Appendix B

NAME:_____ AGE:_____ SEX:_____
                                                    (M-F)

A. Describe yourself by checking the adjectives that describe what
you are like. Check as many as you wish. Try to describe yourself as you *are*, not as you would like to be.

6	1	Aloof	F3	16	Helpful
5	2	Argumentative	3	17	Inflexible
F1	3	Arrogant	1	18	Insensitive
F3, 3	4	Capable	2	19	Introverted
F4	5	Commonplace	F6, 6	20	Intuitive
F4	6	Conforming	F1	21	Irritable
4	7	Conscientious	3	22	Kind
2	8	Curious	F5	23	Mannerly
4	9	Dependent	F1	24	Masculine
4	10	Efficient	F6	25	Nonconforming
1	11	Enduring	F4	26	Not artistic
5	12	Energetic	1	27	Not cultured
F6	13	Feminine	F4	28	Not idealistic
F3, 3	14	Friendly	2	29	Not popular
F3	15	Generous	6	30	Original

* The number opposite an item indicates the type assessed by the item.
All items are weighted +1. To score, simply add together all the correct
responses for each type. All items are scored for both sexes unless they are
preceded by an F. Such items (F) are scored for females only.

F2 31 Pessimistic
5   32 Pleasure-seeking
F2 33 Precise
F6 34 Rebellious
F1 35 Reserved
F2 36 Scholarly
2   37 Slow-moving
F5 38 Social

F5 39 Stable
5   40 Striving
F5 41 Strong
4   42 Suspicious
F2 43 Thorough
1   44 Unassuming
6   45 Unconventional

B. Rate yourself on each of the following traits as *you really think you are* as compared with other people of your age. We want the most accurate estimate of *how you see yourself*. Circle the appropriate number.

		Top 10 Per Cent	Above Average	Average	Below Average
1	Absent-mindedness	0	0	1	1
6	Artistic ability	1	1	0	0
4	Clerical ability	1	1	0	0
4	Conservatism	1	1	0	0
3	Cooperativeness	1	1	0	0
6	Expressiveness	1	1	0	0
5	Leadership	1	1	0	0
3	Liking to help others	1	1	0	0
2	Mathematical ability	1	1	0	0
1	Mechanical ability	1	1	0	0
6	Originality	1	1	0	0
5	Popularity with the opposite sex	1	1	0	0
2	Research ability	1	1	0	0
2	Scientific ability	1	1	0	0
5	Self-confidence (social)	1	1	0	0
1	Self-understanding	0	0	1	1
3	Understanding of others	1	1	0	0
4	Neatness	1	1	0	0

C. Indicate the importance you place on the following kinds of accomplishments, aspirations, goals, etc.

		Essential	Very Important	Somewhat Important	Little Importance
4	Becoming happy and content	1	1	0	0
1	Inventing or developing a useful product or device	1	1	0	0
3	Helping others who are in difficulty	1	1	0	0
2	Becoming an authority on a special subject in my field	1	1	0	0
1	Becoming an outstanding athlete	1	1	0	0
5	Becoming a community leader	1	1	0	0
5	Becoming influential in public affairs	1	1	0	0
4	Following a formal religious code	1	1	0	0
2	Making a theoretical contribution to science	1	1	0	0
2	Making a technical contribution to science	1	1	0	0
6	Writing good fiction (poems, novels, short stories, etc.)	1	1	0	0
1	Being well read	0	0	1	1
4	Producing a lot of work	1	1	0	0
3	Contributing to human welfare	1	1	0	0
6	Producing good artistic work (painting, sculpture, decorating, etc.)	1	1	0	0
6	Becoming an accomplished musician (performer or composer)	1	1	0	0
5	Becoming an expert in finance and commerce	1	1	0	0
3	Finding a real purpose in life	1	1	0	0

D. From the following list of 12 famous people, check the *one* whose life you would most like to emulate.

_3_	1. Jane Addams	_1_	7. Thomas Edison
_4_	2. Bernard Baruch	_6_	8. T. S. Eliot
_1_	3. Admiral Byrd	_5_	9. Henry Ford
_5_	4. Andrew Carnegie	_6_	10. Pablo Picasso
_2_	5. Madame Curie	_4_	11. John D. Rockefeller
_2_	6. Charles Darwin	_3_	12. Albert Schweitzer

E. Circle *L* for those school subjects you like and *D* for those you dislike.

L	D			L	D		
F6, 6	4	1. Art			1	5. Industrial Arts
F4		2. Business		F5		6. Modern History
F2		3. Chemistry		2	5	7. Physics
F1		4. General Science		F3, 3		8. Social Studies

F. I most enjoy the following *(circle one)*:

2	Reading and thinking about solutions to problems	1
4	Keeping records and doing computations	2
5	Holding a position of power	3
3	Teaching or helping others	4
1	Working with my hands, using tools, equipment, apparatus	5
6	Using my artistic talents	6

G. My greatest ability lies in the following area *(circle one only)*:

4	Business	1
6	Arts	2
2	Science	3
5	Leadership	4
3	Human relations	5
1	Mechanics	6

H. I am most *incompetent* in the following area *(circle one only)*:

3	Mechanics	1
5	Science	2
1	Human relations	3

6	Business	4
2	Leadership	5
4	Arts	6

I. Which one of the following activities, if you must perform it, would you find most frustrating or would make you feel the most uncomfortable? *(Circle one only):*

5	Having a position of little responsibility	1
F3	Preparing a textbook on some abstract topic	2
F1	Taking patients in mental hospitals on recreational trips	3
1	Teaching others	4
F6, 6	Keeping elaborate and accurate records	5
F4, 2	Leading or persuading others about a course of action	6
F3, 4	Writing a poem	7
F5, 3	Doing something requiring patience and precision	8
F2	Participating in very formal social affairs	9

VOCATIONAL GOALS

J. Complete the following statements as explicitly as you can:

1. My present career choice is (if possible name an occupation: _____
   (Code response according to Appendix A)

2. If I could not have my first choice *(above)* I would select the following occupation: _____
   (Code response according to Appendix A)

3. If I could not have my first two choices, my third choice would be: _____
   (Code response according to Appendix A)

(5) 4. I have been elected to one or more social, political, or academic offices. *(Circle one):* 0 1 2 3 4 5 6 7 8 9 *or more.*

(2) 5. I have received one or more awards or honors for my academic achievement. *(Circle one):* 0 1 2 3 4 5 6 7 8 9 *or more.*

(4)   6. I have received one or more awards, honors, or special recognition for my business accomplishment. *(Circle one)*: 0 1 2 3 4 5 6 7 8 9 *or more.*

(3)   7. I have received one or more awards, honors, or special recognition for civic, religious, or welfare services. *(Circle one)*: 0 1 2 3 4 5 6 7 8 9 *or more.*

(1)   8. I have received one or more awards, letters, honors, prizes, or special recognition for my athletic ability. *(Circle one)*: 0 1 2 3 4 5 6 7 8 9 *or more.*

(6)   9. I have received one or more awards, honors, or special recognition for my artistic, musical, or literary accomplishment. *(Circle one)*: 0 1 2 3 4 5 6 7 8 9 *or more.*

10. List below all the vocations you have ever considered in thinking about your future. List the vocations you have daydreamed about as well as those you have talked to others about. Try to give a history of your tentative choices and daydreams. Put your present choice on line 1 and work backward to the first vocation you ever considered.

Vocation   At About
                                            What Age?

*(Code responses according to
Appendix A)*

1. _____   _____ _____
2. _____   _____ _____
3. _____   _____ _____
4. _____   _____ _____
5. _____   _____ _____
6. _____   _____ _____
7. _____   _____ _____
8. _____   _____ _____
   _____   _____ _____

Index

ABCDEFGHIJ   7069876